About The Authors

John C. Friel, Ph.D., is a psychologist in private practice in St. Paul, Minnesota; Director of the St. Paul/Minneapolis Lifeworks Clinic, an intensive, short-term treatment program for Adult Child, Co-dependency, addiction and compulsivity issues; and adjunct Associate Professor of Psychology at St. Mary's College Graduate Center in Minneapolis. Dr. Friel earned his B.A. in psychology from the University of San Francisco in 1969, and his Ph.D. in psychology from West Virginia University in 1976. He is a nationally recognized author, trainer, speaker and consultant in the areas of dysfunctional family systems, co-dependency, adult child issues, stress and addictions; and has worked in these areas with the University of Minnesota Medical School, the Gillette Company, Graco Corporation, NCR/Comten, the Minnesota State Bar Association and numerous other corporations, state agencies, treatment centers, hospitals and small businesses. A native of Marin County, California, Dr. Friel has lived in Minnesota since 1973.

Linda D. Friel, M.A., C.C.D.P., specializes in therapy for Adult Children, Co-dependency issues and for Survivors of Physical, Sexual and Emotional Abuse. She designed and implemented one of the first hospital-based co-dependency treatment programs in the United States, and is also a nationally recognized author, trainer and consultant in the areas of dysfunctional families, co-dependency, adult child issues and addictions. A native of Minneapolis, Linda earned her B.A. from Mankato State University in 1971, taught special education classes for eight years and earned an M.A. in Counseling and Psychological Services from St. Mary's College in Minnesota in 1980.

Adult
CHILDREN

The Secrets of
Dysfunctional Families

John C. Friel & Linda D. Friel

Health Communications, Inc.
Deerfield Beach, Florida
www.hcibooks.com

Library of Congress Cataloging-in-Publication Data

Friel, John C., 1947–
   Adult children.
1. Adult children of alcoholics.   2. Adult children of narcotic addicts.
   3. Problem families.   I. Title.   II. Title: Dysfunctional families.
   HV5132.F75   1988   362.2'92   87-25037
   ISBN-13: 978-0-932194-53-4
   ISBN-10: 0-932194-53-2

Publisher: Health Communications, Inc.
         3201 S.W. 15th Street
         Deerfield Beach, FL 33442-8190

Cover design by Justin Rotkowitz
Interior formatting by Dawn Von Strolley Grove

Dedication

This book is dedicated to our family system. To our parents, Elden and Alice Friel and Lloyd and Phyllis Olund; to our brothers and sisters, Bill and Nancy McIntyre, Rich Friel, Steve and Margo Bateson; and to our nieces and nephews, Brian and Carrie McIntyre, John Michael, Mark and Mary Friel. And especially to our children, Kristin, Rebecca and David that their lives may be full and warm and true.

Acknowledgments

We would like to thank all the friends, mentors and colleagues who have shared in and contributed to our professional development and personal recovery: Terry Kellogg, Robert Subby, Lawrence Murphy, Robert Milligan, Lawrence and Sandra Weiss, John Nesselroade, John Cone, Charlie Olsen, Walt Ayotte, Bill Byxbee, Richard and Maureen Gevirtz, Diane Naas, Suzanne James, James Maddock, John Nolan, Richard V. Anderson, Arlene Katchmark, Mary Pietrini, Mary Bell, Lynn Brennan, Lynda Winter, Stan Huff, Evelyn Leite, Linda Murdock, Ken Adams, Bruce Smoller, Virginia Leone and Chuck Ellwanger.

Special Thanks

Special thanks to Arlene Katchmark for her tireless contribution to the preparation of this manuscript.

Preface

The examples and case studies used throughout this book are composites of individuals and families with whom we have worked over the years. The details and specifics of the cases, such as geographical location, job descriptions and names, have been changed for purposes of anonymity. In all other respects these are very typical cases of Adult Children.

Throughout this book we have tried to use case examples that typify different symptoms and addictions so that the reader can get a feel for the variety of dysfunctional lifestyles that develop in Adult Children. By no means have we been able to exemplify in the case studies all of the possible dysfunctional lifestyles and symptoms that can occur. In truth, there are as many case examples as there are people.

As we try to stress throughout this book, recovery is not something that can be done alone; and in many cases, it cannot be done without professional help. A book such as this is written to provide what we feel can be helpful information as part of a much more comprehensive program of recovery.

We must note that self-help books can become an addiction in and of themselves, and that at some point we must get on with the painful business of actually living our lives differently, rather than just thinking or learning about how that might be.

Finally, we cannot stress enough that this book is for *you*. It is not for your husband, wife, lover, children, boss or employees. One of our definitions of co-dependency is "The-Chase-Your-Spouse-Around-The-House-With-A-Self-Help-Book" Syndrome. Recovery from Adult Child issues is a personal experience. The most powerful way to help others into their own recovery is to simply live your own life of recovery. Your own recovery will be well under way when you truly trust that your own example is the most powerful way to help others.

John C. Friel, Ph.D.
Linda D. Friel, M.A., C.C.D.P.

Contents

Part I

Adult Children

Its inhabitants are, as the man once said, "Whores, pimps, gamblers and sons of bitches," by which he meant everybody. Had the man looked through another peephole he might have said, "Saints and angels and martyrs and holy men," and he would have meant the same thing.

from **Cannery Row**
by John Steinbeck

1

Introduction

In July of 1985 thousands of people from all over the world descended on Montreal, Canada, to celebrate the 50th anniversary of perhaps the most successful worldwide organization in existence. This organization, which has no formal leadership and no political affiliations of any kind, was founded by two "failures," and has grown to become the most successful group of its kind in history. It does not accept outside financial support from any foundations or corporations, and it never has. Yet it has a membership of millions of people in over 135 countries. It does no formal promotion of any kind. It does not have marketing personnel. It does not allow its members to use its name for personal promotion of any kind.

In fact, all of its members must remain anonymous, for all practical purposes. According to one of this organization's statements on this issue, "Our public relations policy is based on attraction rather than promotion; we need always maintain personal anonymity at the level of press, radio and films. Anonymity is the spiritual foundation of all our traditions, ever reminding us to place principles before personalities."[1] This successful worldwide

---

[1] These are the 11th and 12th Traditions of Alcoholics Anonymous, reprinted with permission of Alcoholics Anonymous World Services, Inc.

organization, as you may have guessed, is Alcoholics Anonymous.

The history of A.A. is a fascinating study for anyone interested in successful social movements or organizations, regardless of whether or not one "buys" the A.A. philosophy. Despite the tremendously rapid cultural changes that we have experienced since 1935, A.A. has managed to survive and grow. It has weathered the "good times" of the 50s; the upheaval of the 60s; the sexual revolution of the 70s and the "new me generation" of the 80s. In fact, like cancer-fighting cells in the human body, it is starting to spread even more, and it is changing shape as well.

The original 12 Steps of A.A. have been modified slightly to fit a number of other dysfunctional lifestyles. There is Gamblers Anonymous, Narcotics Anonymous, Cocaine Anonymous, Overeaters Anonymous, Bulimics Anonymous, Spenders Anonymous, Parents Anonymous (for recovering child abusers), Smokers Anonymous, Workaholics Anonymous, Debtors Anonymous and Fundamentalists Anonymous (for people trying to break free from destructive religious orientations), Co-dependents Anonymous and Adult Children Anonymous (for adult children of dysfuctional families).

Are these just passing fads? Is A.A. "in" now because of all the awareness we have about chemical dependency? Will it die out as we find new ways of treating emotional and behavioral problems with drugs or behavior modification?

We don't think so. There is a saying in A.A. which says, "If it works, don't fix it." Fifty years of success is a tough track record to dispute. We don't think so because these groups and programs modeled after them are meeting a fundamental human need that all Americans are hungry to get met— the need for healthy intimacy. The need for a place to go where one can talk, share oneself, listen, learn from others and then simply leave at the end of the hour with no strings attached. No politics. No obligations. No one saying, "Okay, I gave you this, now you owe me that."

The 12 steps of A.A. or any other 12-step group do a few simple things very well. They *offer* (not demand) a simple program of living that will, over the long haul, help us to correct the crazy painful ways that we learned to live in this world as we were growing up in our own families. Painful ways that our parents learned from their parents, and they from theirs.

In the year of A.A.'s 50th anniversary, we find a new organization coming into its own at a national level. The National Association of Children of Alcoholics, along with Adult Children of Alcoholics 12-Step groups, based on the original 12 steps of A.A., emphasize bringing hope and help to children *and* adults who grew up in alcoholic homes or other chemically dependent family systems, and they are growing at an astronomical rate.

We also find one of the bestsellers of 1985 being the first-person accounts of famous people's struggles to recover from the ravages of chemical dependency (Dennis Wholey's *The Courage to Change).* Popular articles in newspapers and magazines seem to be zeroing in on chemical dependency and the family system dynamics that go along with dysfunctional and unhealthy dependency in general. And it is this latter issue to which we have devoted this book.

As countless professionals in our field are at last beginning to recognize, it's not just the alcoholic or cocaine addict in the family who has a problem. Even if there is no chemical dependency in the family, the entire family can operate just like an alcoholic family if the rules that govern the system are the same. In other words, it is not just Adult Children of Alcoholics (ACoAs) who can profit from a 12-step group. It is Adult Children of Dysfunctional Families (Adult Children) who can profit, too.

This book is for, about and by Adult Children of Dysfunctional Families. It is written in response to scores of clients with whom we have worked over the years who ask, "Isn't there anything written on this stuff, the way that you've explained it to me?"

It is written to help those of us in recovery remember what our recovery is about and why recovery is a *process* rather than an event. It is written for those of us who are still in the dark—skeptical, angry perhaps, or just plain lost and searching for some kind of a clue as to why we feel the way that we do.

It is written, above all, to shed if nothing more, a flicker of light on the family dynamics that lead so many of us into an adulthood of addiction, depression, compulsion, unhealthy dependency, stress disorders, unsatisfying relationships and lives of quiet desperation.

2

Two Stories

The "Subtle" Family

Frank Davis is a 35-year-old executive for a large California electronics firm. He earned a bachelor's degree in computer science from the University of California, worked as a systems analyst for five years and then went back to school to earn an M.B.A. Shortly after landing his first job with his current employer, he met Tina, who was also a student in business administration and who shared many of the same interests as Frank.

By the end of their master's program, they were married. Three years later they had two small children and one on the way. Tina had decided to defer her career to stay home and raise a family, and Frank's career took off like a rocket. He and Tina had all of the trappings of the successful young couple —a house in Marin County, summer home at Lake Tahoe, two BMWs in the garage and membership in an exclusive country club. They were regular churchgoers and active in the community. Everyone looked at them as the perfect couple.

Frank's childhood was seemingly uneventful. The third of five children, he was born as his father's career as a surgeon was beginning to take off. Frank was a high achiever in school and seemed to take a particular shining to mathematics, which pleased his parents. He was active in sports, attractive and popular with his classmates. Frank's mother was the perfect surgeon's wife in those days—beautiful, poised, charming and a pillar of the community in her own right. Although they had a housekeeper, his mother did not idle her days away. She ran Boy Scout and Girl Scout troops, belonged to the hospital auxiliary, and both she and her husband belonged to a study group at their church. They were a successful, devout and highly visible family in the community, and Frank was proud to be a part of it. He knew that his success was in keeping with the family tradition of excellence.

Frank's father could best be described as "solid." He was a steady, stable, conventional man and, like many surgeons, was a perfectionist. Sometimes Frank's mother would laugh at how "predictable" Dad was, teasing him that she could throw away all of the clocks in the house and just tell time by the regularity of his schedule when he was home. They saw themselves as a loving family, although not openly affectionate very often, owing to their Norwegian heritage on his mother's side and on her father's side of the family. But no matter. They knew that they loved each other, and knowing it was enough, they said.

Frank experienced success after academic success as he breezed through high school and college. And with each success came more praise and adulation from the family. "You're a Davis, no doubt about it," his father would say proudly with each new achievement. By the time he met Tina, Frank had established himself in the world of work and felt up to the task of carrying on the family traditions with his own family. Tina was proud to be a part of it and thrived on the glory she earned as each of the three children was born. At the age of 33, with six years of marriage under his belt and his wife and babies safely at home in the nest, Frank Davis' life began to change.

The changes were very subtle ones at first. He and Tina chalked it up to the "thirties crisis" they'd been reading about in popular books and magazines. After all, their lives had been a whirlwind of accomplishment and activity almost from the day they married. But the changes came anyway, and they didn't leave.

It began with an occasional gnawing feeling in the pit of his stomach as he drove to work, his mind buzzing with ideas for the new project he was directing. Just as quickly, he would dismiss the gnawing feeling and throw himself into the project with renewed vigor, the thrill of success overpowering the nagging little doubts and fears that occasionally crept into his consciousness. At the end of the day he would share a quiet meal with Tina and then go over his plans for the next day's work, then shower and fall off to sleep nestled in Tina's loving arms.

This pattern went on for several months: the nagging little gnawing feeling followed by the thrill of the project, followed by quiet evenings with Tina. Their weekends were usually filled with social gatherings and trips to the lake with the children. But the feelings didn't go away. And by that fact alone, they began to haunt Frank. His dreams became disturbing. He became distracted. Then he became mildly irritated at times, which really frightened him. No Davis worth his salt let little things irritate him, let alone gnawing little feelings.

Throughout this initial period, Tina maintained the role of the supportive, tolerant wife. She managed the household, stayed involved in the community, acted the part of the charming hostess and quietly nurtured Frank in the evenings. But eventually whatever it was that was eating at Frank, finally began to eat at her, too.

While Frank could not identify the source of his gnawing, Tina could. It frightened her even more so because she could. For months she had shoved the feelings away until she could do it no longer. What she was feeling was resentment toward Frank, and as she told herself over and over and over again, that was unthinkable! And because it was unthinkable, because her marriage as she viewed it was the perfect marriage and all that she had ever hoped to attain, she entered deeper into a trap with Frank, nearer and nearer to the center of the trap where they would together step on the mechanism that was to snap the jaws of the trap around their deeply entwined lives.

She followed Frank's lead and poured herself into community activities and jaunts and projects with the children and all of their friends. She received praise after praise from friends and community leaders. She was elected to local boards and committees. Her life became a dizzying whirlwind of success, after wonderful success as a parent, friend and innovative community leader.

At last their oldest child, Jason, entered the trap with them. At the age of seven he began to have problems in school. He was bright and both he and the teachers knew it, yet he began to forget to bring home his school-work for his mother to see. He started bullying other children and acting up in class. He did lots of things to get attention but very few of them were constructive.

When the school finally contacted Tina, she reacted coolly and calmly, stating that *her* son wouldn't be acting that way were it not for insensitive teachers. Within days, she transferred Jason to a private school which was funded in large part by Frank's electronics firm, and things seemed to be under control.

Somewhere inside of her complex brain, a tiny little voice tried to speak to Tina. It was the voice of a little girl; an innocent, spontaneous voice. It was clear, and bright as a diamond, but very weak. It kept saying over and over, "Something's wrong, Tina. Something's wrong."

With her friends and relatives and community colleagues loudly prais-ing her accomplishments on the outside, this little voice kept getting stronger and stronger on the inside. It created an internal battle that finally burst forth one Thursday evening as she and the three children sat quietly eating dinner.

Frank walked through the front door, bursting with enthusiasm about the new contract that he had landed just as Jason abruptly and loudly knocked over a glass of milk as he reached to hit his little sister in the shoul-der. For a split second, they were in a surrealistic state of suspended anima-tion. Tina's eyes froze in shock then darted instantly from Jason to the milk, and finally rested in an icy glare, fixed and penetrating, on Frank. Her hands and face flushed with heat as a burst of primitive fury exploded inside her.

All eyes were riveted on her as she leaped to a standing position, picked up her plateful of food and hurled it at Frank, grazing his forehead and splattering a mixture of asparagus and Hollandaise sauce over his suit and the foyer behind him. She screamed with a rage she did not know existed in anyone.

"Don't ever walk into this house again with that stupid grin on your face!"

For another split second there was total silence, and then Tina simply crumpled into a ball on the dining room floor and began to sob deep heartrending sobs that began in the very center from which the little girl spoke to her and echoed eerily out into the night. She lay there and sobbed and sobbed and sobbed for what seemed like forever, and then she quietly walked upstairs to their bedroom and closed the door, locking it behind her. The children began to cry in fear and helplessness. It was the first time they had seen either of their parents do more than the occasional snapping that all parents do to each other. Frank just stood there in the foyer in absolute shock and disbelief. The trap had snapped around all of them months before—it was only now that they could all touch the pain. The pain was now real. They could smell it and taste it and see it and breathe it. This was to be the beginning, or the end, and not one of them knew which it was to be.

Frank tried to quiet the children as best he knew how. Then he tried to get into the bedroom to talk to Tina, but the door remained locked the rest of the night. "Please just go away," she would whimper whenever he tried to get into the bedroom.

He slept on the couch in the living room that night, awakening several times with a knot in the pit of his stomach.

Tina came down in the morning and fixed breakfast for Frank and the children. They didn't talk at all over breakfast and the clink of the silverware on the china was empty and loud. Frank left for work dazed, tired and feeling lost. The children went to school with a sickness in their stomachs that lingered throughout the day.

Tina cried most of the morning, alone and confused. The child inside of her had turned into a monster and she didn't know what to do with it. In sheer panic and desperation, she picked up the telephone book and found the name of a psychotherapist. She spent most of the afternoon battling with herself over whether to call or not. But as the time neared for school to be out for the day, she picked up the phone and dialed the number.

"I don't know what's the matter with me," she told Frank and the children that evening, "but I'm going to get some help to find out. Something is terribly wrong and I can't live this way anymore."

There are innumerable schools of psychotherapy and theories about why human beings run amuck for apparently "no reason," and the formal diagnosis that Tina's psychologist put on the insurance form for reimbursement came right out of the Diagnostic and Statistical Manual of the American Psychiatric Association (DSM-III), but her brief summary notes, which she scribbled on Tina's intake form, said it best:

> Thirty-three-year-old white female, married seven years, three children. Husband workaholic, wife experiencing severe

co-dependent rage, depression, guilt and loss of identity following months of compulsive activity and several years of active
denial.

Frank was a workaholic, and Tina Davis did the only thing she knew
how to do in the face of a loved one's addiction—she let her own addiction
escalate.

At first she was addicted to Frank, waiting up for him when he was continually late at the office, reheating meals she had prepared hours before,
nurturing and supporting Frank and his addiction, and denying the slowly-
building resentment that at last burst forth in a flash of rage.

In the end, she joined him in his addiction, taking on more and more
work herself to try to blot out the frightening feelings that kept coming to
the surface, and that she had never been taught how to deal with herself.
And it is no coincidence that as the little child inside of her began to speak
more clearly, her actual biological child began to speak up in the only way
that he knew how—by *acting out* the unspoken, unrecognized tensions in
the family while he was at school and at home.

The fate of the Davis family has yet to unfold fully. Tina has entered into
long-term therapy to begin the process of discovery and relearning necessary for her to avoid stepping into her own dependency traps again. Frank
and the children, along with Tina, are all in family therapy.

Frank's awareness of the underlying dependencies in his own life is still
very dim, and although he does not say it openly, he still believes that the
problem is basically Tina's. The family rules and bonds that gradually led
him into his success-oriented work addiction are seductive and powerful,
and the denial system that he took on by living in a family that "knows they
love each other" but that has trouble expressing it spontaneously runs deep.

In an addictive system of any kind, every member of the system is pro-
foundly affected. For true health to occur in the new system that hopefully
emerges from a crisis such as this, every member must change if the system
is to remain intact.

Sometimes, when only one or two members of a system become healthier, their only alternative to maintain their own health is to leave the system.

The "Obvious" Family

Sandy Dorset grew up in a suburb of Boston, the oldest of five children. Her father started drinking heavily soon after he married Sandy's mother, and by the time Sandy arrived on the scene, he had been laid off from his job in a parts supply house due to financial problems within the company. Although he had a bachelor's degree from a small state college in the area, his unresolved emotional difficulties and untreated alcoholism kept getting in the way of his finding a decent job.

Sandy's mother began working part-time as a licensed practical nurse to help ends meet while her husband went from job to job looking for the "right break."

During the next six years four more children were added to the Dorset household, and the combination of financial and childbearing stresses produced an explosive and draining situation at home. By the time Sandy was five years old, her father had become physically abusive to her mother, and was extremely verbally abusive with the children.

Sandy recalls cowering in the corner of the living room, the younger children huddled around her for protection, as her father screamed and yelled, then hit her mother. These episodes would be followed by a few days, or even weeks of relative calm, then the whole cycle would repeat itself.

Once, Sandy's mother tried to get help for the family by talking to a friend who was in Al-Anon, and whose husband was making a successful recovery from alcoholism, but this enraged her husband so much that she never spoke to her friend again for fear of what her husband might do to her or the children.

And so the Dorset family remained violently trapped throughout Sandy's childhood, the periods of chaos interspersed with periods of gut-wrenching silence, with everyone holding their breath and walking on eggshells in hopes that it would get better—but it never did.

Sandy learned to exist in this system by building a protective barrier around herself. When she was little, she played alone in her room for hours and hours, creating a fantasy world of imaginary friends and places in her mind. As she grew older, it became easier for her to block out the pain by staying away from home as much as she could, although this tore her in two directions at once, because a part of her felt the need to be at home to take care of her younger brothers and sisters.

Like many children in alcoholic families, she became a star student academically, and she kept the family secret well. Everyone knew that the Dorsets were poor, but Sandy always managed to have a freshly pressed blouse to wear and she was always polite and eager to please. She never mentioned the horrible events that took place at home. Family honor is family honor, no matter what happens.

In high school Sandy began to gain weight and had difficulty taking it off. By the time she entered the two-year nursing program she was 100 pounds overweight, but she never let it get her down. She excelled in the nursing program and was working full-time only three weeks after graduation.

At the age of 25 Sandy Dorset started dating a young man who she felt must have been sent to her from heaven. He was gentle, caring, even nurturing, and he was attending the university to become a counselor. They never talked about her weight problem, but in the back of her mind she worried that it would eventually turn him off. Nevertheless, they dated continuously for several months, and then decided to get married.

Two years into the marriage, Sandy gave birth to a baby girl. By this time her husband was working long hours as a counselor with disadvantaged youth, so she cut back her nursing duties to half-time to spend more time with the baby. It was also at this time that her husband had an affair with a friend of hers. Although she had sworn from as far back as she could remember that she would never drink any kind of alcoholic beverage, she began to drink to medicate the pain of a life that seemed to be crumbling all around her.

As her marriage deteriorated, she drank more and more to deal with the horror of realizing that *the whole pattern of her childhood was repeating itself.* She became desperate and suicidal. And she was lucky ... because the hospital staff where she was admitted after taking an overdose of sleeping pills was able to pick up on her chemical dependency very quickly.

Distraught but relieved to have someone finally take care of her the way no one ever had when she was growing up, Sandy Dorset gladly accepted the hospital's recommendation that she enter chemical dependency treatment, and it was there that her life truly began.

Her road to recovery has not been an easy one. As with many alcoholics, stopping the alcohol intake itself was not nearly as hard as she thought it might be, but the pain of dealing with the underlying dependencies (co-dependencies as we now call them), with the tremendous amount of re-learning that has to take place and of having to face head-on the emotional tortures of growing up in an abusive alcoholic family was at times more than she thought she could bear. Her husband had divorced her by now, and yet she kept on working and struggling and confronting her fears, angers and hurts.

She began attending Adult Children of Alcoholics Al-Anon groups in addition to her A.A. groups and continued her gradual but steady climb out of the depths of despair. With each new step out of the darkness, she seemed to find healthier and healthier friends. Her weight, which had climbed to 150 pounds above normal at the height of her crisis, slowly began to come off. Her daughter was growing up to be a happy, well-adjusted child. For the first few years following treatment, Sandy dated irregularly but never seriously. She had a job and her daughter to look after, and her own recovery to manage. In her early thirties she met a man who truly was different. He was caring without taking responsibility for her problems. He got crabby on occasion but it never went beyond that. They would fight about things but would get them resolved and go on, none the worse for wear. They each spent time alone as well as together. And they each had their own A.A. meetings to go to.

Sandy and her second husband have been married now for 15 years. While they have had their ups and downs as any couple does, the night-mare of her first life has turned into something quiet, comfortable and whole. Although the nightmare will never completely leave her, it has taken a realistic place in her past and serves as a constant reminder that whenever she gets under too much stress, or feels too insecure, or feels like her emotions are overwhelming, there is a healthy way for her to respond. Sandy Dorset is living now.

3

Who Are We?
What Are Our Symptoms?

Who *are* these adult children of dysfunctional families of whom we speak? Where do they live? How much money do they earn? What kinds of problems do they have? Who are these people anyway?

"They" are us.

At least 90–95% of us, as we will show later on. Many of us are adult children of alcoholic parents who fit the characteristics listed in Janet Woititz' bestselling book *Adult Children of Alcoholics* (Woititz, 1983). Or we are women or men who "love" too much, as described by Robin Norwood (Norwood, 1985).

As Terry Kellogg (1986) states: many of us are not just the victims of alcoholics or child abusers or spouse beaters, many of us become alcoholics, child abusers and spouse beaters ourselves whether we are male or female.

As adult children of dysfunctional families we operate in a world of extremes—always seeking that healthy balance, the Golden Mean, but always seeming to fall short of the mark. The pendulum swings to one extreme and we feel lonely, isolated and afraid. We tire of this, and it swings to the other extreme, where we feel enmeshed, smothered and angry. Then it swings back

17

again. This is true in many areas of our lives, until we get into a solid recovery program.

On our way to conduct a workshop in Texas a few months ago, we generated a list of our own which might help to begin to describe the troubles that plague Adult Children:

1. We are people who hit age 28 or 39 or 47 and suddenly find that something is wrong that we can no longer fix by ourselves. It may coincide with the normal stage crises described by Levinson (1978), Gould (1978), Sheehy (1974) and others, but its intensity and accompanying pain and confusion suggests that there are Adult Child issues beneath the surface.
2. We are people who gaze at our peers on the street or at a party and say to ourselves, "I wish I could be like her or him."
3. Or we say, "If only he knew what was really going on inside of me, he'd be appalled."
4. We are people who love our spouses and care deeply for our children, but find ourselves growing distant, detached and fearful in these relationships.
5. Or we feel that everything in our lives is perfect until our sons or daughters become chemically dependent, bulimic, run away from home or attempt suicide.
6. We are the underemployed, never seeming to be able to achieve our true work potential—stuck in jobs we loathe because we're confused, afraid or lost.
7. We are the chemically addicted, the sexually addicted and the eating disordered.
8. We are the migraine sufferers, the exercise bulimics and the high achievers with troubled marriages.
9. We are the social "stars" who feel terribly lonely amidst our wealth of friends.
10. Some of us grew up in chaotic families and were weaned on alcoholism, incest and physical, emotional and spiritual abuse.
11. Some of us are especially paralyzed now because the dysfunction we experienced was so subtle (covert) that we can't even begin to put a finger on what it was that happened to us.
12. Some of us were compared to a brother or sister who did well in school.

13. Others were led to believe that we could only have worth and value if we became plumbers or doctors, electricians, lawyers or psychologists.

14. Some walked on eggshells throughout childhood because the family was poor, Dad worked two jobs, Mom raised five kids pretty much by herself, and everyone was tired and on edge most of the time.

15. Many of us were emotionally neglected because no one was physically there for us; or because they were there for us with material things but were absent emotionally.

16. Some were spoiled and smothered out of misguided love; seduced to stay in the nest years after our friends had gone out into the world and begun their adult lives.

17. Many of us are afraid of people, especially authority figures.

18. Others of us frighten people, especially our loved ones, and demand that our loved ones live in our isolated worlds— controlled completely by us.

19. We are people who despise religion or who despise atheism.

20. We let others use and abuse us or we use and abuse others.

21. We are people who have only anger, or only sadness, or only fear, or only smiles.

22. We try so hard that we lose; or try so little that we never live life at all.

23. We are men and women who look "picture perfect" (Fry, 1987).

24. We are men and women who hit skid row and feel like we finally belong somewhere.

25. We have depression or we have rage.

26. We think ourselves into emptiness or we feel ourselves into chaos.

27. We are on emotional roller-coasters or in emotional vacuums.

28. We smile while slamming the kitchen cabinets shut because we're really angry or we slam the cabinet angrily when we're really sad.

29. We abuse ourselves but take care of everyone else.

30. When we are unhappy, we are terribly afraid to acknowledge it for fear that someone will find out that we are human; or even worse, that we are even here at all.

31. We have trouble relating to our sons, our daughters or both.

32. We can make love, but we can't get emotionally close or we can't make love at all.

33. We constantly watch others to try to find out what's okay and what isn't.
34. We feel less than some and better than others but we rarely feel like we belong.
35. We get stuck in lives our hearts never chose.
36. We hang onto the past, fear the future and feel anxious in the present.
37. We work ourselves to death for unknown purposes.
38. We are never satisfied.
39. We fear God or we expect God to do it all for us.
40. We fear or hate people who are different.
41. We get into friendships that we can't get out of.
42. We get hooked on things.
43. We project our inner conflicts onto our children.
44. We are embarrassed about our bodies.
45. We don't know why we're here.
46. We suffer as much as we can.
47. We see a police car and feel like we've done something wrong.
48. We sacrifice our dignity for false security.
49. We demand love and rarely get it.
50. We wish for things instead of going out and getting what we want or need.
51. We hope for the best, expect the worst and never enjoy the moment.
52. We feel like the rest of the human race was put here to make us feel intensely uncomfortable while eating at a restaurant alone.
53. We ask "Where's the beef?" but unlike Clara Peller in the TV commercial, we aren't getting paid to ask. And nobody answers.
54. We run away when we fall in love or we abandon ourselves for the relationship.
55. We smother those we love, we crush those we love or both.
56. Some of us will turn the tide of history by our actions, and some of us will live in obscurity.
57. We will grow up to hate our parents, or we will keep them on the pedestals that we put them on when we were little, but we will rarely let them be the error-prone humans that we all are.
58. We feel guilty about the way our brothers or sisters were treated compared to us or we feel jealous and slighted about the way they were treated compared to us.

59. We hate Dad and overprotect Mom or we hate Mom and overprotect Dad.

60. We were sexually abused by someone when we were five years old but blame ourselves, telling ourselves that we should have known better at age five.

61. Some of us had a parent who was chronically ill when we were growing up.

62. Some of us had a parent who was mentally ill when we were growing up.

63. Some of us had no parents at all when we were growing up.

64. We are survivors who deep down inside pray that someday life will be more than just mere survival.

65. We are lovers of life whose little child is locked inside of us, waiting to be set free.

Regardless of our symptoms or circumstances, we are Adult Children of Dysfunctional Families because:

Something happened to us a long time ago. It happened more than once. It hurt us. We protected ourselves the only way we knew how. We are still protecting ourselves. It isn't working anymore.

Symptoms of Adult Children

The symptoms that we develop as a result of what happened to us run the gamut of psychiatric and stress-related disorders, from substance use disorders and other addictions to depression, phobias, anxiety, personality disorders, sexual dysfunction, intimacy disorders, overactivity, eating disorders, compulsive behavior and obsessions. We will be the first to agree that not all of these problems in all cases have as their primary cause some kind of dysfunction in our families. Alcoholism, schizophrenia, certain kinds of depression, some forms of anxiety, and some types of obesity all seem to have well-documented biological roots. But it is curious to us that in all our years of doing therapy, we have encountered few if any alcoholics, for example, who did not also come from dysfunctional families and who were not also re-enacting that dysfunction in their own current family systems.

In fact, we can think of two people who came from healthy families but seemed to inherit the biological predisposition to become hooked on alcohol, and they handled the problem in a very functional way. They both said to themselves, "I think I'm getting addicted to this stuff." They talked to their family and friends about it, and then they sought help to stop the addiction. The difference for most of us is that we're too dysfunctional to do that.

The symptoms that we develop have certain characteristics that seem to hold true for most Adult Children.

Our symptoms . . .

1. Are part of our denial system.
2. Give us the illusion that we are in control.
3. Started out as a normal response to some perceived stress.
4. Form as a way of protecting ourselves from a pain that we as children had no power to remove.
5. Are about the denial of feelings.
6. Are intimacy and relationship "blockers."
7. Are about shame.

Our symptoms are born out of emotional *denial* and they serve to maintain that denial. They are ways that we allow ourselves to live one kind of life while convincing ourselves that we have a very different kind of life. And while they serve to give us the *illusion that we are in control,* they are in fact clear indicators that what we have really done is to give up healthy control of our lives to something outside of ourselves.

By becoming trapped in an addiction or phobia, we actually trade true control over our lives for the illusion of control. It is this illusion of control that makes giving up our symptoms so frightening.

The sex addict truly and sincerely believes that if he or she gives up unhealthy sex, life will crumble in chaos. The relationship addict, most often addicted to a person who is himself an addict, sincerely believes that if he or she tries to change in healthy ways, life will fall apart. The exercise bulimic who keeps his weight under control by running, who finds his only sense of "psuedo-inner peace" by running, and who shows all the signs of withdrawal when he isn't able to run, truly and sincerely believes that his life will not be worth living without the ability to run.

Our symptoms all *started out as a normal response to some perceived life stress.* It is our opinion that the breeding ground for them was introduced in childhood, when we were learning how to live with other people. When those family systems in which we grew up had some kind of dysfunction, whether it be obvious (overt) as it was in Sandy's case, or subtle (covert) as it was in Frank's case, it is normal, logical and reasonable for a child in that family to protect himself or herself. Just as the physical body will isolate an infection and protect the rest of the body by creating a cyst around it if it is left untreated for too long, our childhood minds will isolate the source of psychological pain in a safe blanket of denial to maintain some kind of balance.

These symptoms form as a way of protecting us from a pain that we as children had no power to remove. From the early beginnings of denial grows a pattern of splitting ourselves in two, like Sandy did. She was the competent, high-achieving child on the outside and the frightened, hurt, lost little child on the inside. The longer this dysfunction went untreated, the more adept she became at denying her true feelings. And the more we deny our feelings, the worse we feel.

And so our symptoms are about the *denial of feelings*, too. We shut off the hurt and the fear. We bask in the praise of "outsiders" who can only see the public image that we present. We take pride in being "the strong one" or "the rebel" or the "cutie pie" and all the while we are dying inside because we feel that no one really knows who we are, and they probably don't. Thus our symptoms are also *intimacy or relationship disorders.*

By supporting our denial and by helping us to maintain our "family se-crets," they also keep us from ever getting close to anyone else in healthy ways. We always have to keep our guard up in the hopes that no one will find out what's really inside, which means that our symptoms are also about *shame.* They are about the shame of "being found out," of being "discovered," of being emotionally naked in front of others and being laughed at, criti-cized or rejected.

The list of symptoms that can develop in Adult Children of Dysfunc-tional Families is quite long. In many of us, there are several of these pres-ent at the same time. We have never met a compulsive overeater, for example, who does not have an unhealthy dependency on food. We have rarely seen a spouse of an alcoholic who is not literally addicted to the relationship with their spouse, who is not compulsive in several other areas of life, who does not have an unhealthy dependency on other people or things and who does not have problems with depression.

It is not the label one puts on people that determines what kind of family problems they will have or what kind of parents they will make. It doesn't matter to the child whimpering in her bedroom after being screamed at by her frustrated lonely mother whether or not her mother is labeled a relationship addict, a co-dependent or a compulsive overeater. What matters to that child is the fact that Mom and Dad aren't happy, that Mom and Dad scream at her all the time, that Mom and Dad put her in the middle of their fights and that Mom and Dad won't let her feel her real feelings.

While our list is not all-inclusive, we believe it does provide a picture of what happens to so many of us Adult Children.

Some Symptoms Developed By Adult Children

Emotional/Psychological

1. Depression
2. Anxiety/panic attacks
3. Suicide or suicidal thoughts
4. Obsessions and compulsions
5. Chemical addictions
6. Low self-esteem
7. Personality disorders
8. Phobias
9. Hysteria
10. Sexual dysfunction
11. Suspiciousness
12. Intimacy problems
13. Dissociation
14. Flat affect
15. Difficulty concentrating
16. Excessive anger

17. Low frustration tolerance
18. Passive/aggressive personality
19. Extreme dependency
20. Inability to be interdependent
21. Inability to play or have fun
22. Inability to be assertive
23. People-pleasing
24. Approval seeking
25. Identity confusion

Physical

1. Chemical dependency
2. Eating disorders
3. Accident proneness/chronic pain syndrome
4. Tension and migraine headaches
5. Respiratory problems
6. Ulcers, colitis, digestive problems
7. Constipation/diarrhea
8. Sleep disorders
9. Muscle tension
10. TMJ (Temporomandibular Joint Disorder)

Because they tend to be so common for Adult Children, we will take a brief but closer look at addictions, compulsions, unhealthy dependencies, depression, stress symptoms, phobias and anxiety.

Addiction

In the narrowest sense, an *addiction* is a physiological dependence on some substance, in which the dependence has got out of control and is affecting the daily functioning of the addict in some pretty serious ways. This definition, of course, would leave out the broader uses of the term as in work addiction, love addiction, television addiction, etc. We would prefer to use "addiction" more broadly defined because that is the way that it is being used quite often now. We suspect that the distinction between an addiction and an unhealthy dependency may simply be one of degree anyway.

Compulsion

A *compulsion* is something we do that we do not feel we are able to control or stop, but gives us the *illusion of being in control.* The "out, out, damned spot" compulsive hand-washing to try to remove some imagined sin from one's hands is a classic example of a compulsion, as would be getting up in the night seven or eight times to check to see if you locked all the doors and windows. Clinicians speak of compulsive overeating, compulsive gambling or compulsive cleaning and spending. Sound familiar? Am I a compulsive gambler or am I a gambling addict? Or does it really matter what we call it, as long as we know that it's something out of control that is doing us and others harm?

Unhealthy Dependencies

Unhealthy dependencies grow out of our normal dependent state as infants. We are born totally dependent upon our parents for our survival. Without them feeding us, nurturing us and taking care of us when we are sick, we would literally die. Thus our dependency needs are rooted deeply and firmly in terms of absolute survival.

As we grow older, these needs take on subtler and subtler forms. At the age of six, for example, it is possible for us to actually survive on our own, as many children have to do in impoverished countries, although we do not survive well at this age without continued help from adults. At the age of 15, we can survive quite well on our own, at least in terms of meeting basic biological and safety needs. But what about the less obvious emotional needs that we have? The needs that are less tangible but powerful nonetheless? It is most often these needs that don't get met in dysfunctional families, which means that we are launched into adulthood with a reservoir of unmet needs.

One of the major tasks of growing up is to learn how to become interdependent with others. Interdependence means being one's own person, being able to maintain a clear and separate identity from others, while still recognizing the need for help and support from others. It also means being able to get that support in healthy rather than destructive ways.

Am I interdependent if I have a "lot of friends" but start to feel that I do too much for them and don't get enough back? Am I interdependent if, like Sandy, I am high-achieving, responsible, and competent at work but feel like no one ever knows the real me? Or am I simply displaying the underside of unhealthy dependency?

Friel (1982) wrote of a *paradoxical dependency,* in which the person having this problem appeared self-reliant and independent on the outside but was floundering on the inside. Paradoxical dependency is one form of an unhealthy dependency. Looking strong and "together" on the surface, while having unhappy relationships and low self-esteem underneath, is a clear sign of unhealthy dependency.

Unhealthy dependency means that the attachment that we have to a substance, a job, a person, a pet or whatever is getting in the way of our happiness and contentment. These attachments, like addictions, prevent us from hearing the little child inside of us who wants his or her needs met in healthy ways, and who wants to be set free. They keep us in denial, they keep us from forming healthy attachments to friends and lovers. Beneath them is the same fear, sadness, hurt, loneliness and anger that is beneath addictions and compulsions.

Unhealthy dependencies prevent the formation of healthy interdependence, and thus are destructive to us. And as many experts know too well, unhealthy dependencies, left untreated, will often deteriorate into full-blown addictions under normal life stresses.

Depression

Depression is something that we all experience at one time or another. It includes feelings of low self-esteem, sadness, feeling "blue" or "down," being tired, apathetic, eating a lot or not much at all, sleeping a lot or not much at all and so on. Many long-term depressions are due to imbalances of neurotransmitter substances in the brain, so that the brain is not getting stimulated enough.

Antidepressant medications have been very helpful in treating these kinds of depression. But we see so many cases of depression that are treated only with medications, when the true underlying problem is a lot of unresolved "junk" from childhood.

We get depressed when we don't know how to get what we need in life. We get depressed to punish others. We get depressed to get others to help us, so depression can be a way of achieving power over others. We get depressed when we're afraid to express our anger. There are all kinds of depression.

For every person who is not on antidepressant medication and should be, it is our hunch that there are several more who are on them and won't need to be once they recognize and deal with the reality of being an Adult Child of a Dysfunctional Family.

Stress Symptoms

Stress symptoms, such as migraine or tension headaches, many forms of temporomandibular joint disorder (TMJ) (sore jaw joints from grinding the teeth), ulcers, colitis, skin disorders, backaches, muscle tension problems, asthma, etc., are extremely common among "Adult Children".

They are common because when we "hide out" and try to stuff what we believe are "inappropriate" feelings, they come out sideways anyway. Instead of crying, we get headaches. Instead of telling our spouse that we don't like to go shopping, we go anyway and get stomach pains. Instead of admitting that we're tired, we work ourselves into the ground compulsively to show how strong we are, and develop hypertension. Our bodies react to things around us whether we like it or not. It is up to us to express those reactions in healthy, not dysfunctional, ways.

Phobias

Phobias are irrational fears that keep us from going about our day-to-day affairs with comfort. Severe phobias can keep us from going about our day-to-day affairs at all. We develop fears of people, of going outside the house, of working or of going to school. While the specific phobia may be attached to a single traumatic event, it is often the rules in our family system that keep us from overcoming the phobia. And those same rules can help the phobia to expand and grow into other irrational fears that paralyze us even further.

Anxiety

Anxiety symptoms include trembling or shaking, dizziness, chest pain or discomfort, faintness, fear of dying or going crazy, hot and cold flashes, tingling in the hands or feet, sweating, heart palpitations, jitteriness, jumpiness, tension, feeling tired and worn out, eyelid twitches, restlessness, cold clammy hands, dry mouth, upset stomach, frequent urination, diarrhea, high resting pulse rate, worry, fear, hyper-attentiveness, distractibility, difficulty in concentrating, irritability and impatience.

That's a long list of symptoms, and most of them can also be caused by physical problems, which is why it is strongly advised that you get a complete physical exam before assuming that it is anxiety.

On the other hand, we see many people who go from doctor to doctor and one expensive test to another looking for a physical cause of their symptoms, when what is really happening to them is that they have some deep-seated emotional pain that they are not looking at. When they face the pain, the symptoms begin to slowly disappear.

Our general advice on symptoms is to get a complete physical examination first, to help rule out physical causes. Should you seek psychotherapy, we recommend that you tell your therapist that you also want to explore possible family dysfunction causes for your symptoms, in addition to just getting medication or behavior modification treatment.

In our view, symptoms are either biologically caused, or they are there for a protective reason that is most likely due to family dysfunction.

4

Some Hooks:
Addictions in
Particular

Because addictive and compulsive patterns of living are so common among Adult Children of Dysfunctional Families, we would like to take a brief diversion to identify what some of these hooks are.

An estimated 28 million Americans have at least one alcoholic parent. More than half of all alcoholics have an alcoholic parent.

One in three families report alcohol abuse by a family member. In up to 90% of child abuse cases, alcohol is a significant factor (National Association of Children of Alcoholics Charter statement).

Experts suggest that 80 million Americans are overweight (Turner & Helms, 1987).

One in three adults still smoke cigarettes (1987 Gallup Poll), millions of people drink coffee, many addictively so, and injuries from jogging number in the thousands.

Before their highly addictive nature was recognized by the medical and psychotherapeutic community, prescription tranquilizers, such as Librium and Valium, trapped untold thousands in addiction.

The average child watches six to eight hours of television every day. By the time he graduates from high school, the average child has spent more hours in front of the television set than in school.

It took two years to sell the first 5,000 copies of the A.A. *Big Book*, the bible of A.A., first printed in 1939. Now it takes two days (A.A. World Services, 1985). This, of course, is an uplifting and joyful statistic because it shows us how many people are now getting help for a disease that was once thought untreatable, but it also shows how hungry we are for help with our addictive processes.

We could compulsively cite statistics for another 20 or 30 pages to make our point, but we won't. We aren't here to use scare tactics or to tear down American society. There are plenty of other societies struggling with their own addictive problems. But we *do* feel that it is necessary to at least frame addictive agents in broad terms.

To begin, we will simply list for you some of the more common agents to which we can become addicted based on our clinical experience, current research and our own personal experience. Feel free to add to our list or take issue with it if you wish.

alcohol	jogging
prescription drugs	reading
nonprescription drugs	speed/danger
illegal drugs	nicotine
food	caffeine
television	relationships
sex	power
work	sleep
spending	gambling
stress	cults

The first thing to notice about our list is that with perhaps one or two exceptions, there is not one item on our list that is harmful or dangerous in and of itself. There are plenty of people who go to Lake Tahoe, Las Vegas or Atlantic City for a weekend of gambling and entertainment and never have a problem with it. There are plenty of people who drink alcohol moderately, and for whom alcohol never becomes a problem. Even stress, in and of itself, is not dangerous. In fact, without some stress in our lives, life would become very boring. So it is not the addictive agent itself that is the focus of our message, *except that it is very important to realize that addiction can happen to us in more ways than one.*

Just because you don't drink alcohol does not mean that you are free from addiction. You could have *all* of the traits of an addict—the denial, the discomfort with intimacy, the need for unreasonable power and control, the inability to let go, the inner torment, the insecurity masked by grandiosity and so on—*without being an alcoholic.*

And before you start pointing fingers at yourself or someone else because of our list, remember that just because you like jogging or sex or television does not mean that you have an unhealthy dependency on them. Also keep in mind that we are each unique in important ways, too. Watching television may be a healthy diversion or form of entertainment for you, but be a demonic trap for your spouse or children. Your boss's relationships may be healthy, while yours are bordering on being addictive. His work may be challenging and stimulating while his assistant's work may be addictive and compulsive. The proof is not in the pudding; in this case it's in the one who is eating the pudding.

Perhaps the following brief descriptions will begin to help shed some light on this distinction.

> Jim has one or two drinks after his long workday, then eats dinner with his family. On weekends he and Barbara usually entertain at home or go out with friends, and he finds that a few glasses of wine and some after-dinner drinks help loosen him up to really enjoy the weekend. All of their friends drink, and Jim only gets "drunk" a couple of times a year. He knows that he really doesn't have a problem anyway, because he tried to stop drinking last year and was able to go two months without a drink. Jim has a successful career, a beautiful wife and two wonderful children. Jim is an alcoholic.

> Katherine has one or two drinks after her long workday, then has dinner with her family. On weekends she entertains at home or goes out to dinner with friends. She, too, has a couple of glasses of wine with dinner when she goes out. She has never

tried to quit drinking completely because it has never occurred
to her to do so. Katherine is not an alcoholic.

Sue has been running 30 miles per week for the past several
years. Every couple of years she trains for and runs in a
marathon. She is proud of her physical fitness and can't imagine what it would be like to not be able to run anymore. In fact,
her morning run comes before anything else and when her
schedule becomes disrupted for some reason, she is irritable and
crabby for most of the morning. Sue is a running addict.

Frank runs 40 miles a week, running at least one marathon
every year. He, too, is proud of his stamina and conditioning.
When he discovered that he would have to stop running because
of a knee injury, he was disappointed and "down" for awhile but
he eventually bounced back and is on an even keel again. He has
been thinking lately about taking up swimming to get his aerobic exercise each day. Frank is not a running addict.

Bob watches television with his family every night, starting
with the evening news and ending with a late night movie.
While Bob is watching, other family members will be watching,
too, if they're interested in the show. But Bob watches no matter what. His wife jokes about being a "television widow," but
she's not laughing on the inside anymore. Bob is a television
addict.

Mary watches television every night or so, depending on
what's on, but it is never a very high priority for her. Even if she's
in the middle of a program and someone calls her up to go out,
it doesn't bother her to turn it off. Sometimes she'll go for days
without watching anything at all. Mary is not a television addict.

As you can see from the above examples, it is not the amount, necessarily, that determines the addiction. In some cases, amount by itself will be a
clear diagnostic indicator, but it won't always. One of the statements that will

get an Alcoholics Anonymous group laughing harder than anything else is when a diagnosed alcoholic says, "But I only get drunk a couple of times a year!" This also brings up the important advice that as we think about our own dependencies and possible addictions, *we must not compare ourselves to someone else's patterns of use.*

The best way to look at our own patterns of addiction is to look at a typical list of the symptoms and indicators of addiction used by professionals to determine *whether* we are addicted and *how strongly* we are addicted. We believe that addiction is on a *continuum*, and that if you suspect that you or someone close to you is addicted to something, you should seek professional help in determining a diagnosis. The following are some of the major indicators.

1. **Preoccupation With The Addictive Agent:** Thinking about it, talking about it, looking forward to it, being distracted because of it, not being able to "be" with others because of the preoccupation. It is this aspect of addiction that makes intimacy difficult, if not impossible after awhile, because the addiction becomes our *primary relationship.* We are more interested in watching TV, having sex, drinking, running, gambling, etc., than we are in being with the people we once loved.

2. **Increased Tolerance For The Addictive Agent:** We need more and more of the chemical or experience to achieve the desired effect. The more we use it, the less the effect seems to be. There is also increasing frustration with the tolerance build-up, in that the increased usage causes deeper and deeper shame, guilt and remorse.

3. **Loss Of Control:** We can't have "just one." We try to have periods of abstinence; or we have "white-knuckle" abstinence during which times we are irritable, angry, lonely and isolated. We say that this is the last day we'll act out compulsive sex, or watch TV all day, or drink, or use Valium, but we get up the next day and start all over.

4. **Withdrawal:** When we stop using whatever it is we're addicted to, we have symptoms of withdrawal, such as irritability, depression, moodiness, tearfulness, anger, hostility, etc. This goes as well for addictions other than chemical addictions. Families asked not to watch

TV for a month often have the same symptoms if they happen to be addicted to it.

5. **Sneaking:** Hiding bottles, shamefully buying pornography and hiding it in one's car, under one's bed. Having a few drinks or pills before going out for the evening to be sure that there's enough in the bloodstream in case there is no opportunity to have more later.

6. **Denial:** To be discussed at length in a later chapter. It includes defensiveness about use and one's symptoms, as well as the consequences of one's actions for self and others around us; as if the world is crumbling around us and we're saying, "Problems? What problems? Everything's fine!" Or we might say, "Addiction? Hell no, I'm not addicted. I'll be fine after I get done with this big project. It's just the stress I'm under right now that's getting to me."

7. **Personality Changes and Mood Swings:** Up, down, up, down, up, down. Angry, syrupy-sweet, then angry again. Moody, temperamental, irritable, sad, hyperactive, elated, then back to sad again. In some, these swings are very obvious. In others, they are much subtler.

8. **Blaming:** It's everyone else's fault. The kids are too spoiled. The spouse isn't attentive enough, or sexy enough, or enough of a hard-worker. The boss is a jerk. The doctor who examined me is incompetent. There is a powerful inability to accept responsibility for one's own life with this symptom.

9. **Blackouts:** With chemical addictions, these occur when we can't remember what we did while we were under the influence—we don't remember driving home or how we got to bed or what we said to that woman at the party last night. With other addictions we have "dissociative blackouts," i.e., we dissociate while using or while preoccupied and don't remember things. We daydream, "space out," "go into the ozone" for awhile.

10. **Physical Symptoms:** These will depend upon the addiction. With non-chemical addictions, they are most often the stress disorders, such as headaches, ulcers and the like.

11. **Rigid Attitudes:** Black-and-white thinking; intolerance of others' opinions, compulsiveness, all-or-nothing thinking.

12. **Loss of Personal Values:** We stop caring as our addiction progresses. We don't take care of ourselves. We hang around with people who are our "inferiors." Our boundaries break down and we do things which we would never do prior to the acceleration of our addiction—sexual things, inconsiderate things, hurtful things, illegal things.

13. **Disability and/or Death:** Death comes either through physical damage due to a drug or chemical, or through stress-related illnesses, such as cancer or heart attack or stroke or through eventual suicide. We suspect that a large number of alcohol-related traffic fatalities are a form of suicide.

In looking at most addictive agents, there are usually two factors involved in the addiction: *the biological or physical addiction* and *the social/emotional addiction.*

Most experts will now agree, for example, that many alcoholics have a genetic predisposition to becoming physically addicted to alcohol. The brain and blood chemistry of alcoholics is different than in non-alcoholics, even *before* they started drinking. There is also pretty strong evidence that alcoholics metabolize alcohol differently than non-alcoholics, producing an opiate-like substance in their brains after consuming alcohol.

In looking at "love addictions," it is intriguing to consider the recent discovery of a special neurotransmitter in the brain that seems to exist in much higher amounts when we are "falling in love." It appears that the rush of energy, excitement and feelings of ecstasy and well-being that occur when we fall in love are due in large part to this neurotransmitter substance (neurotransmitters are the chemicals that send the electrical impulse from one nerve to the next in the brain and other nervous system parts). In the case of "falling in love," the more of this substance present, the stronger the feelings of euphoria and well-being.

As the newness of the relationship wears off, so does the accumulation of this substance, resulting in boredom, sadness or even depression, which of course can be "cured" by falling in love again. Perhaps some people who become addicted to multiple serial relationships, who fall in and out of love all of the time, are actually addicted in part to this neurotransmitter substance.

The *social/emotional* factors in addiction seem to be common to all addictive agents, regardless of brain chemistry or body physiology, and it is these factors over which we have much more control at the present time, and on which we wish to focus. In almost every case, these factors include:

1. Temporary anxiety reduction.
2. Temporary stress reduction.
3. Temporary feelings of power and well-being.
4. Avoidance of true feelings.
5. Avoidance of crucial life problems and developmental tasks.
6. Avoidance of intimacy.

Because of the very nature of addictive processes, these benefits are not long-lasting. The well-being we feel while drunk wears off, leaving us in worse shape than when we started drinking the day before. We are left with a hangover, tremendous guilt and shame.

The anxiety reduction, or reduction of boredom and frustration that occurs when we go on a spending binge, goes as quickly as it came, leaving us guilty, nervous, shameful, and anxious about how we will pay our next month's bills.

We may get a rush of euphoria and happiness as we walk out the door with a date to whom we are addicted, but when that date is over and we find ourselves pining away by the telephone waiting for him or her to call again, whatever sense of false security we may have had will be long gone. In its place will be feelings of worthlessness, anxiety, frustration and despair.

Put simply, these addictive agents serve to fill in developmental gaps in us quickly and temporarily and by using them often, *we never get the chance to fill in the gaps permanently*.

Multiple Hooks

Sandy was alcoholic and food addicted. Frank was a workaholic, and as it turned out in the course of therapy, he was sexually addicted as well. In our clinical experience, it is rare for someone to have a single addiction.

The reason for this is simple, actually. Addictions are really symptoms of a deeper underlying dependency that evolved out of our family systems during childhood. The more dysfunctional the family, the deeper the underlying dependency problems that exist in us. The deeper the underlying dependency problems, the more they pervade every aspect of our lives, because the pain inside of us is stronger and more frightening, and it takes stronger defenses to deny that pain and try to hide it from others. It is only logical that a combination of alcohol, food, cigarettes and compulsive perfectionism will serve to help us hide our pain more than if we used only food or only alcohol.

Remember, too, that even to the untrained observer, someone who is addicted to all of these things may obviously have a problem.

But to the addict who doesn't get a lot of feedback from other people because they are afraid of it, it is easy to fool himself into believing that no one knows "his secret."

By the same logic, dealing with multiple addictions is no different from dealing with just one. Once we break through the initial denial and defenses to treat the most harmful addiction first (such as alcohol), it is much easier to treat the other ones later while recovering from an addictive lifestyle. The alcoholic may say to herself at first, "I know I have to quit drinking, but I know I'll have to find something to replace it."

Once recovery has been in process for a couple of years, she actually finds it easier to think about giving up the next addiction. As addicts, we think in terms of how much of what kind of outside agent we can rely on. As people in healthy recovery programs, we begin to think of how healthy we are and how we can get even healthier. It is as if our entire logic system changes.

A warning is in order here, too. Early in recovery, it is very predictable that we *will* replace one addiction with another. The recovering food addict may begin compulsively running, only to find that running is making her no more peaceful inside than food did. This simply means that recovery is still very new, and that the person doing it has more and deeper work to do with the underlying pain. The goal of recovery is to produce inner peace and a clear identity, free from addictive agents. The first step in recovery is to remove the addictive agent so that the true underlying dependency can be felt, touched, seen and dealt with openly.

Interlude

5

The Bear

Once upon a time there was a big Brown Bear who lived peacefully in the woods near a clear rushing stream. He liked where he lived. He liked the fresh clean air, the abundance of fish in the nearby stream, the dappled sunlight beneath the tall pine trees, the open meadows and the cool damp forest. Every day was filled with quiet time snoozing in the sun on his favorite granite rock by the stream, the challenges of searching for food and romping with his mate.

One day as he was ambling down to the stream for a drink of clear icy water, something happened. WHACK! A searing pain pulsed through his foot. He lunged forward to escape. THUD! He was trapped to the earth by a pair of steel jaws and a thick metal chain pounded deep into the earth.

"No!" shouted the big Brown Bear. "It's a bear trap."

His paws weren't really built to spread the jaws of a bear trap, and his brain wasn't really built to figure this out at all. He was in a bad situation.

After several hours of painful struggle, the big Brown Bear had mangled his foot almost to shreds. There was blood everywhere. He called for his mate, who finally heard his calls, but there was nothing she could do either. So she sat patiently next to him to give him comfort, crying quietly, and hoping for a miracle.

Finally, after several more hours, his mangled foot jerked free from the trap, and he crawled sadly away from that place and back into the woods. His mate stayed behind for awhile to try to understand how this had happened, but nothing came to her. Her brain wasn't really designed to figure these things out either.

At last, she returned to their den, where the big Brown Bear was nursing his mangled foot as best he could. They stayed up most of the night, discussing what had happened to them that day, but neither of them could make head nor tail of it. And so with what brain capacity they did have, they simply decided never to return to that place in the woods again. And so they didn't.

Part II

Family Roots

"A safe but sometimes chilly way of recalling the past is to force open a crammed drawer. If you are searching for anything in particular, you don't find it, but something falls out at the back that is often more interesting."

J. M. Barrie, from the dedication
to his first edition of **Peter Pan**

6

Family Systems:
Structure, Function,
Roles, Boundaries

Perhaps the most important contribution to understanding the dynamics underlying "Adult Child Issues" has come from the field of family systems (e.g., Bowen, 1978, Minuchin, 1974, Satir, 1967). Because of its importance, we want to spend some time here just going over the basics of family systems so that you can begin to get a framework for understanding what happened in your family.

Every system has a *structure* and a *function*. Our nervous system is made up of a brain, spinal cord and nerves that carry messages to and from the brain. Its function is to allow communication to take place within the body, and between the body and the outside world. The circulatory system is composed of the heart, veins, arteries and capillaries and its function is to circulate blood throughout the body to deliver food to the cells and to carry away waste products from the cells. A business or other organization has a structure, too, which includes a president, a vice president, managers, other employees and so on. Its function will depend upon its corporate goal.

For example, its function may be to produce television sets, sell them, make a profit and provide jobs for its employees and goods for society to buy.

Each family has a structure and a function, too. The *structure* of a family system is made up of the individual members of the family, including parents, children, grandparents, aunts, uncles and perhaps others who live with the family for an extended period of time. Part of the family structure is also the boundaries and relationships among and between family members: who is allowed to communicate with whom, and so on. A family in which Dad is closer to oldest daughter than he is to Mom has a very different structure than one in which Dad is closest to Mom, even though the number of -family members is the same.

When a therapist helps you construct a genogram of your family system, he or she is helping you discover the structure of your family (McGoldick & Gerson, 1985.)

In the next chapter we will provide you with an example of a simplified genogram that has helped scores of our clients begin to understand what has happened to them as they grew up in their families. But for now, we would like to offer the analogy used by internationally recognized family therapist Virginia Satir and further developed by her student and colleague, Sharon Wegscheider-Cruse (Wegscheider, 1981), well-known for her work with chemically dependent family systems.

The analogy is that of a *mobile*. As you imagine a mobile suspended from the ceiling of your living room, notice how all of the separate pieces of the mobile hang magically suspended in delicate harmony and balance with each other. Although each part of the mobile might be a separate, fragile piece of crystal or polished metal, the mobile as a whole seems to be at one with itself—one beautiful, whole work of art. If you bumped against one element of the mobile, it may move with a burst of energy and unpredictable motion—but it does not move by itself. Although it appears to be a separate, solitary piece of crystal or metal, it is connected nonetheless to the rest of the mobile by wire or string. And thus, whatever energy it picks up from you will be transmitted to the rest of the mobile, even though the effect may be subtle and nearly imperceptible.

In other words, whatever happens to one part of the mobile affects the other parts of the mobile. If you stop bumping into the mobile, something else very predictable will happen, too. Each of the individual, autonomous pieces of that mobile will return to precisely the same spot that it was in before you bumped into it. The mobile is a "whole" work of art that "wants" to be what it is, the way it "should be," the way it was "meant to be." So it returns to its original form, hanging silently where it began, a whole made up of individual parts, each in its own place, carrying out its function of giving us joy and a sense of beauty. It is truly a brilliant metaphor that Satir provides us.

The mobile tells us a lot about principles of systems. It tells us that:

1. Systems have a definite structure to them. Each piece of the mobile has its place. It would not be the "same" mobile if we were to rearrange the pieces.

2. The whole is greater than the sum of the parts. The mobile is more than just pieces of strings or wire and pieces of metal or crystal. It is a work of art with its own identity, defined by how all of the parts are arranged.

3. Changes in one piece in the system affect all of the other pieces in the system (but not necessarily in the same way).

4. Systems always try to return to their original state. This is the principle of dynamic homeostasis or balance. It would not be the "same" mobile unless after I bumped into it, it returned to the same place that it was before I bumped into it.

The Unhealthy Family System

Let's look at an example that hits closer to home. Let's make each piece of that mobile a member of a family instead of a piece of metal or crystal. One piece is Dad, who works very hard and also watches a lot of TV. Another piece is Mom, who works a lot and worries about the kids. Another is oldest son, who gets good grades and is the valedictorian of his high school. A fourth is middle sister, who is "nice" and quiet, and praised for "not being a bother." Lastly comes little brother, who is cute and sassy and funny. This mobile is in balance. It has a structure. It is a family, which is more than just a Dad or a Mom or a big brother, a middle sister or a little brother. And like all systems, if one member gets "bumped," it affects all members. And when one member gets "bumped," everyone, unconsciously, without malice, tries to get him or her back into place.

So Dad works and watches TV and Mom works and worries. Dad and Mom don't take care of themselves. Dad and Mom don't nurture their marriage. Oldest son works harder and harder to get good grades and be a star on the football field. Middle daughter works harder and harder to fit in, be "nice" and not make waves. Youngest son gets cuter and cuter.

Dad and Mom begin to feel empty in their marriage. They lose touch with each other. This creates stress. No one talks about it. The stress remains. Mom worries more about the kids. Dad watches more TV. Oldest son wins more honors. Middle daughter gets nicer. Little brother picks up on the marital stress and gets drunk with his 8th grade friends. Dad gets concerned. Mom worries a whole bunch. Older brother gets another "A" to make sure the family is doing okay in spite of the stress. Middle sister gets nicer, quieter and tries to fit in more. And then little brother gets caught using drugs.

The mobile has been bumped! Something is causing chaos. We know what it is. We can fix it. We are a system. We are a family. Let's rally together, get closer, identify this problem, analyze it, troubleshoot it, discuss it, make a list of options, huddle 'round, come together and lick this thing! Little brother has a problem, and we won't leave him alone with it. We are going to help him. And so we do. We will seek counseling for little brother.

Because we care, we agree to go to family counseling with little brother because that's what the counselor recommends. We go. The counselor tries to look at the whole family system. He or she starts to focus on Mom and Dad. We wonder why. We just want little brother fixed. There's nothing wrong with anyone else in the family! Why, just look at big brother. He's successful. Just look at middle sister. She's so nice. Look at how hardworking Mom and Dad are. No. It's just little brother. Please fix him.

But it's not just little brother. We can't see that, though, and so we terminate the counseling to reduce our anxiety about having to look at ourselves.

Little brother continues to act out. Eventually he becomes chemically dependent or truant enough or steals enough that he must go to some kind of inpatient treatment. While there, he starts to feel better because someone is hearing him, someone is asking him to be responsible for his own behavior without putting him in a dysfunctional system at the same time.

Thirty days later, little brother is doing much better. He goes home. Everyone thinks that the problems are over. But they aren't, because no one else in the system has done any work on *their* problems. Dad and Mom haven't looked at their shaky marriage. Big brother hasn't looked at what a burden it is to have to be a "star" all the time. And middle sister hasn't looked at the huge toll she is paying for being "nice" all the time. So more than likely, the system will return to its original state. In this case, it means that little brother will continue to provide his service to the family, which is to act out its pain so that no one else in the system has to admit that there's anything wrong.

This happens all the time unless the whole family eventually gets help. Little brother will continue to act out in more and more serious ways until he either grows up and leaves home and gets help, or until he gets put in jail, or dies of alcoholism, suicide or in a reckless auto accident. If he's lucky, when he leaves home, he'll try to get help on his own.

If the family still resists getting involved in treatment, his therapist will recommend that he stay away from the family as much as possible and that he develop a "new" family system to replace the old dysfunctional one. This new system may be a therapy group, a 12-Step group, such as A.A., Al-Anon, ACoA or some other structured support system that follows a functional set of rules in which little brother does not have to "feel crazy" to fit in.

In more and more cases nowadays, what happens is that the entire family does get involved in treatment; and not just for little brother's sake. Enlightened therapists and an enlightened general public are helping families to see that problems like these are really symptoms of problems in the entire family system, and that when one member of the system is displaying a serious problem in adjustment, it means, in most cases, that all of the other members are experiencing problems, too. It's just that these other members' defenses and roles are more socially acceptable and less troublesome on the surface.

The Healthy Family System

The obvious question now is: what happens in a healthy family system? Healthy systems experience stress and problems, too. Mental health does not mean the absence of problems. Far from it. Mental health means the ability to handle problems in a healthy way. A healthy family system is like a mobile, too. But the rules and boundaries and roles and interconnections between family members are different.

In the example given above, Dad and Mom in the healthy family system would probably sit down one day and say to each other, "You know, I've been feeling overworked and kind of distant from you these past few weeks, and I don't like it. In fact, it scares me a little. I don't like what's happening to us and our family. I think we need to make some changes."

Dad might say, "Yeah, I've been in a rut lately. Work, work, work, and then I just sit in front of the tube all night."

Mom would say, "I spend too much time worrying about the kids but doing nothing about it."

They decide to change some things about their marriage. They spend more time together without the television on. They share some of the housework perhaps. Then they talk to the kids about the changes they've been making, and ask the kids how they're doing.

Because they have already recognized and admitted their own stresses, and have then done something to change the situation, they are giving a powerful, clear, healthy message to the kids that change is okay, admitting problems is okay and coming up with solutions is okay. Preaching and demanding is not necessary here.

With this clear permission-giving via their own behavior, Dad and Mom make it very easy for the kids to express their fears and needs and wants.

Older brother might then say, "Yeah, I've been working too hard, too. It's fun to be successful, but I need more time just to socialize. You know, make more friends. Do things just for the heck of it now and then."

Middle sister might say, "My friends all say I'm so nice! But sometimes I think they take advantage of me because I'm too nice. It makes me angry. I think being nice all the time isn't good for me."

And little brother is then free to say something like, "I'm tired of everyone treating me like a toy. I'm little, but I'm not a toy. I have rights and feelings, too. And I want to be more responsible for things around here."

Does this sound far-fetched? Impossible? Contrived? It is not. For purposes of space and time, we have left out the details of how a healthy family negotiates these changes; but what we have just presented here is exactly the kind of process that happens, over a period of time, in a healthy family. The people ultimately responsible for the workings of the family system (the parents) made some healthy changes, and those changes reverberated down through the system in a healthy way; just like the unhealthy denial of problems reverberated down through the system in the first scenario, ending in what is called the "scapegoating" of little brother.

Family Function

The family has several functions that it serves, just as any other system has functions. Many of these functions meet family member's needs. *For example, there are maintenance functions,* in which basic needs such as food, clothing and shelter are met. When the furnace breaks down, someone fixes it. When we outgrow our clothes, someone provides new ones. When we are hungry, someone feeds us.

The family provides for these needs in various ways. Sometimes one family member will provide the money needed to buy most of these things. Sometimes every family member is involved in providing these basic maintenance needs.

The family should also provide safety, warmth and nurturance to its members. Family members in a healthy system will care for each other, provide appropriate touch, laugh together, cry together, share joys together and protect each other from harm.

As psychologist Abraham Maslow has noted, we also have love and belongingness needs, which are quite similar to the ones just mentioned. We need a sense of communion, of belonging to a group or a unit, of being loved and included. A healthy, functioning family will provide these, too.

There is also a need for autonomy or separateness. A healthy family will allow its members to be largely self-determining (depending upon the age of the family member). Children will be allowed to find out what they like and don't like about the world, what they want to do for a living. They will be allowed to have privacy and a sense of uniqueness as well as belonging. Parents will be able to change their minds about things like careers, roles and so on as their needs change or as their personalities develop over time. Parents and children are allowed to love each other without having to be enmeshed and tangled up in each others' lives.

Families also function to promote **self-esteem** *or a* **sense of worth** *in each family member.* This is done by praise, rather than criticism, and by healthy skill-building, rather than relentless pushing and demanding of perfect performance. We believe that each person truly *does* have value and truly *does* have something important and worthwhile to offer to the world and to the family. A healthy family will let each person find and have that sense of personal value, dignity and worth.

Families also get to make mistakes. That's right! Healthy systems have room for human error and imperfection. We get to be naughty now and then, and it's okay. We might call this the "blowing-off steam function." Think of a steam-heating system without a pressure-release valve! That wouldn't be too good, would it?

Families get to have fun. We get to be silly, playful, creative and "let our hair down." This is the "primary process" kind of thinking that Freud spoke of, and which the Transactional Analysts call The Child. Families that allow play to be an important function tend to be much more creative at solving their own conflicts and stresses.

Families have spirituality, too. Whether we know it or like it or not, spirituality is a very important function that a family provides. We aren't talking about formal religion here because we know some very spiritual people who do not belong to a formal religion, and some very spiritual people who do (and vice-versa). By spirituality, we mean our relationship with creation, with the universe, with the ineffable, unexplainable around us, with a Higher Power, with the cosmos, however you describe it. People who learn to let go of what isn't important, and to persevere with what is, very often can do so because of their spirituality.

There are other functions that a family can provide for its members, but let's stop here and see what happens when a family is dysfunctional. What happens then is that we get stuck in dysfunctional roles.

Dysfunctional Roles

Those needs and functions just listed are things that each family member should be getting. In a dysfunctional family, those functions are often divided up separately and delegated to one specific family member. Let's take a look at some of the dysfunctional family roles that develop (Wegscheider-Cruse, Satir, Kellogg).

The Do-er

The Do-er does a lot of things. The Do-er provides most or all of the maintenance functions in the family. The Do-er makes sure the kids are dressed and fed. The Do-er pays the bills, irons the shirts, cooks dinner, takes the kids to baseball practice and violin lessons. The Do-er does a lot. But because it is a dysfunctional family, that's about all that the Do-er has the time or energy to do. So the Do-er feels tired, lonely, taken advantage of, neglected and empty. But the Do-er gets a lot of satisfaction out of being so accomplished at his or her tasks, and the family encourages the Do-er either directly or indirectly. And the Do-er's own unhealthy guilt and overdeveloped sense of responsibility keeps him or her going.

The Enabler/Helper/Lover

The Enabler provides all of the nurturance and sense of belongingness in the family. Sometimes this person is also the Do-er, and sometimes not. For the Enabler/Helper/Lover, keeping everyone together, preserving the family unit at any cost (including physical violence or even death) and trying to smooth out ruffled feathers and avoid conflict is the ultimate goal. Fear of abandonment and fear that other family members cannot stand on their own two feet are what often motivates this role.

The Lost Child/Loner

As identified by Wegscheider-Cruse, The Lost Child deals with the family dysfunction by means of escape. But actually, in a sense, this child (or parent) is taking care of the family's needs for separateness and autonomy. This is the child who stays in her room alot. Or is the one who is out in the woods, playing by himself. He or she is alone, but it is not a healthy aloneness. It is a deep loneliness that pervades those who have this role.

The Hero

The Hero provides self-esteem for the family. He goes to law school and becomes an internationally known attorney, but secretly feels awful because he has a sister in a mental hospital and a brother who has died of alcoholism. But he carries the family banner for all the public to see. He makes the family proud; but at a terrible price in terms of his own well-being.

The Mascot

Often one of the younger children, the Mascot provides the humor and comic relief for the family. He or she gives the family a sense of fun or playfulness, of silliness and a distorted type of "joy."

The cost to the Mascot is that his or her true feelings of pain and isolation never get expressed, and he remains an emotional cripple until he gets into a recovery program of his own.

The Scapegoat

The Scapegoat gets to act out all of the family's dysfunction and therefore takes the blame and "the heat" for the family. He gets drug addicted or steals, is the "black sheep," gets in a lot of fights, acts out sexually, etc. The family then gets to say, "If little brother weren't such a delinquent, we'd be a healthy family." The cost to the Scapegoat is obvious.

Dad's Little Princess/Mom's Little Man

This role, as we will discuss later, is a severe form of emotional abuse which many professionals call *emotional* or *covert incest*. This role feels good to a child, who gets to be "a little spouse" to one of the parents in the system. This child does not get to be a child, though, and is actually seduced into the role by a parent who is too afraid and too dysfunctional to get his needs met by another adult. Those of us who were given this role usually wind up getting physically or emotionally abused by others in our adult relationships, because our boundaries were not respected when we were little.

The Saint/Priest/Nun/Rabbi

This is the child who expresses the family's spirituality and is expected to become a priest, a nun, a rabbi or a monk, and not to be sexual. Often the expectation is never a spoken one. It is implied, and is subtly reinforced and encouraged. This child is unconsciously molded into believing that he or she will only have worth if they act out the spirituality for the family. And if they don't, they will have little or no worth.

There are many other dysfunctional roles that we can identify, and many of us "cycle-through" different roles as we grow up in our families. A Lost Child can also be a Scapegoat. A Mascot can become a Hero later on.

People often ask us, "But aren't these roles present in a healthy family, too?" Our answer is always "No!" What *does* exist in a healthy family is different personality types. Sure, one person may be shy while another robust and gregarious. Recent research suggests strongly that this is due to genetic differences between family members.

But does being shy mean being isolated and alone? Isn't there a way for a healthy family to provide all of those needs for a shy child? Of course there is. A shy child can still feel loved and feel like he belongs. He can certainly have a sense of acceptance and worth. He can make mistakes without being abused for them. He can be a separate person without being lonely. He can be spiritual. He can have fun. Don't shy people have fun?

What makes these roles dysfunctional is the very fact that they are roles. Healthy families don't pigeon-hole us into one tiny script. If a "shy person" (as Garrison Keillor of Minnesota Public Radio fame calls them) gets "loud" now and then, who's going to shame her for it? Who's going to say, "Hey, kiddo, your role is to be shy and quiet. So shut up and be quiet so you don't upset the mobile." Would a healthy family do that to a shy child? Not on your life! Only a dysfunctional family would do that.

Boundaries

We are talking about psychological and social boundaries here, although in principle they are the same as the physical boundaries around one's property, city, state or country. For our purposes, we will look at three types of boundaries:

1. Individual boundaries
2. Intergenerational boundaries
3. Family boundaries

Within each type, we can have three boundary states:
1. Rigid boundaries (too strong)
2. Diffuse boundaries (too weak)
3. Flexible boundaries (healthy)

Each individual human being should have a clearly defined boundary around himself/herself, which is like a psychological fence around us, defined by us. This individual boundary lets certain things into our lives and keeps certain things out of our lives.

Figure 6.1. Individual Boundaries

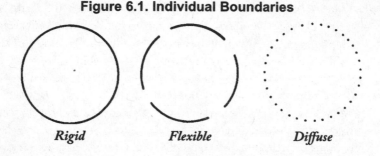

Rigid   *Flexible*   *Diffuse*

When someone asks me to help them paint their house on Saturday, and I decide that I want to use Saturday for rest and relaxation, I am setting a boundary for myself. When they continue to ask, and then resort to guilt and manipulation, they are trying to violate the boundary that I set. They are trying to invade my boundary. This would be an *individual boundary invasion.*

Likewise, if someone tried to make love to me when I said I didn't want to, this would be an individual boundary invasion.

If my boundaries are too *weak,* I will always let anyone do to, or with me, what they wish. I can never say no. If I do this long enough, I will develop serious emotional problems; and eventually I will swing to the opposite extreme and set up completely rigid boundaries, in which nothing gets in *to me* and nothing gets out *from me* to other people. I become an emotional hermit living on an island totally alone. No one can invade my boundaries now, but then who cares? There is no one in my life at all.

After months or years of subtle boundary invasions by a friend or lover, I might scream in desperation, "No, you selfish, manipulative s.o.b., I won't help you paint your house this Saturday or any Saturday, for that matter. In fact, I don't want your friendship anymore and I don't want you coming near my house again!"

This rigid boundary will protect me for a while, but the cost will be too great. Eventually I will become so lonely and isolated that I will allow the swing to the opposite extreme to occur when I least expect it. I will jump at the chance to help someone again someday out of sheer loneliness, with the hope of making a new friend, but with my own growth stifled, that person is likely to use me until I blow up again.

In dysfunctional families, we swing back and forth, back and forth, between rigid and diffuse boundary states, hoping to find some kind of balance. The only true balance, though, happens when we are in the middle of this swing, when we have flexible boundaries. With flexible boundaries, we might say, "You know, I'd love to help you sometime but this has really been a tough week for me. I'm going to have to decline."

It sounds so simple. But it isn't. How many times have you put someone else's needs before your own, only to reach the burnout point soon after that? How many times have you come up with a good excuse for why you don't have to take care of yourself first?

"Yes, I'm exhausted, but after all, he is my best friend." Well, if he truly is your best friend, he'll understand and respect you for setting your own limits.

It is our belief that the underlying reason that we can't set these healthy limits is that we are desperately afraid that we will be *abandoned* if we say "No." *Fear of abandonment is the primary dynamic beneath most dependent and addictive behavior,* in our estimation, and how we get this way has a lot to do with the other two types of boundaries we spoke of.

Intergenerational boundaries are those invisible lines between the parents or other adults in the family, and the children in the family.

Figure 6.2. Intergenerational Boundaries

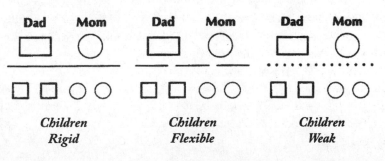

If our parents have difficulty expressing feelings towards us, if they don't know how to show love, if their own individual boundaries are too *rigid,* then this intergenerational boundary will be too rigid also. We will always feel alone as children. Our parents will never be "there" for us, either physically or emotionally or both. They will never play with us. They won't empathize with us. They won't seem to care. It will feel like they are distant and detached from us. It will feel cold and empty in our families. In some families these intergenerational boundaries will remain rigid most of the time. In others, they will swing to the opposite extreme *at times.* In still others, they will be in the opposite extreme *most of the time,* i.e., there will be weak intergenerational boundaries.

With weak intergenerational boundaries, the line between adults and children is very unclear. This is very common in dysfunctional families and is most blatant where incest occurs. When adults have sex with children, the children's individual boundaries are certainly violated, but so is the boundary between adults and children. Whenever we put our children in an adult role, we are crossing this boundary.

Emotional incest is more common than actual physical incest. With emotional incest, we make our children into "little spouses" for us. We lean on them for support. We share our deepest problems with them. We may call them "Mommy's Little Man" or "Daddy's Little Girl." We ask them to fill emotional needs in us that we can't get met on our own. The very thing that they, as children, *need* from us, we ask them to give to us. Sound crazy? It not only is, but it makes for very sick little children, too.

We see this kind of intergenerational boundary invasion happening right after divorce, for example. Moms and Dads cling to their children for the emotional support that they needed from their spouses. And because it makes children feel so important and powerful, and because they are so vulnerable themselves, children become the perfect victims for this kind of emotional incest. It robs the child of childhood. It robs the child of a sense of safety and security, and it teaches the child that the only way he or she can get important needs met is to be a victim. Above all, boundary violations teach us to be victims.

Figure 6.3. Family Boundaries

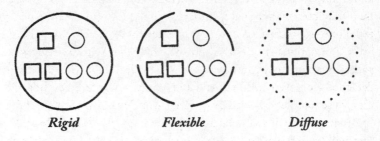

Rigid   *Flexible*   *Diffuse*

Family boundaries are those which surround the family as a whole unit. With a closed family system where the "No Talk" rule is in full force, we speak of rigid family boundaries. It's "us" against the world.

When little Suzy races home to tell Mom how much fun she had at Karen's house because Karen's mom just taught them how to bake bread, Suzy's mom replies coldly or angrily or sarcastically, "If you had so much fun with Karen's mother, why don't you just go live there!" When we see all our friends getting together for a "sleepover" or "slumber party," we want to have one at our house, too; and, of course, with rigid family boundaries, this is not possible. We seldom see any other people in the house. It is as if the entire family lives alone on an island. It becomes very lonely, and eventually very unhealthy.

With diffuse family boundaries, the family has no sense of unity at all. People flow in and out. No one seems to be "in charge." There are no clear limits or rules. It doesn't feel like a family at all. It's more like a bunch of molecules wandering aimlessly about, occasionally bumping into each other but never being able to define where the family ends and the rest of the world begins. "Chaotic" describes this situation well.

Think about your own family when you were growing up. Then think about your pattern of family and friends now. Do you see any parallels?

As we move on to the next chapters, keep in mind these principles of family systems because they tell us about the traps from which we must escape if we are to truly recover from the symptoms of being Adult Children.

7

The Traps Get Set

Is it enough to be able to label our symptoms? We don't think so. We don't think so because we know that it isn't enough just to have this information. Our clients don't get better with just information. Denial systems don't change with just information. Feelings don't get out with just information. What we also need to understand is *the process* by which these symptoms were acquired. They didn't happen overnight. We don't just wake up one day and find that we are now living a painful life. It is a process that takes a long, long time to happen.

Bill's Story

Bill Hopkins entered treatment for sexual addiction[1] at the age of 38, after an intervention that was attended by his wife, his two partners in the accounting firm that he founded, his sister and a friend of his.

---

[1]For an excellent discussion of sexual addiction, see Patrick Carnes' *Out of the Shadows* and Ken Adams' article entitled "Sexual Addiction and Covert Incest" in *Focus On Chemically Dependent Families*, May/June, 1987.

Two years prior to the intervention, Bill's wife became concerned about his sexual acting out. She started to make regular comments to him soon after that. As is often the case, Bill dismissed her concerns with a wave of his hand at first, saying, "Dear, if I really had a problem, I'd do something about it. Really, honey, worry about something else for awhile." Anita kept worrying, though.

Several months later the situation escalated to the next stage. Bill's involvement with pornography and masturbation increased as the pressures from expansion of his business increased. He took on a junior partner, but it didn't help his addiction. Bill grew distant from Anita, and their interactions became either cool and perfunctory, or heated battles and debates. The friction in their marriage became more and more intense, until one Friday night when the trap snapped completely around them.

Anita had been out with a friend for dinner, which she had begun to do more and more out of frustration and helplessness. When she walked through the door at 9:30 that evening, Bill told her that he had contracted a venereal disease and that he couldn't have sex with her for awhile. Anita packed a suitcase, went back to her friend's house, and spent the weekend with her. On Monday morning she filed for a separation. The next day, Bill called her, apologized, and said if she would move back home, he would stop acting out immediately.

Anita moved back into their house and things cooled off for several months. Bill was actually proud that they had been able to work this out by themselves, and Anita was tremendously relieved that she wouldn't have to be watching Bill all the time. Their communication was still a little shaky, but it was improving. About three months before he entered treatment, Bill decided that he had the whole thing under control and that his sexual addiction had only been a symptom of the business pressures that he now seemed to have managed well.

It wasn't long before his addiction had escalated again to destructive proportions. Anita contacted COSA (Co-dependents of Sex-Addicts) and asked for some help. They put her in touch with an intervention specialist who met with her and the other concerned persons who would do the intervention. One week before the intervention was done, they all sat down and practiced how it would be accomplished. When Bill was faced with his wife and friends and the data they presented him, he grudgingly accepted their recommendation for treatment, which was the *beginning* of his and Anita's recovery process.

Admitting a problem like sexual addiction carries with it both a sense of relief and a sense of failure and loss, and one of the goals of treatment for addictions is to educate the family about how the addiction process is acquired. Everyone is asking themselves, "How could this happen to us? *Who* caused this? *Who* is to blame?"

One of the goals of this educational process is to *let* people *see* the dysfunctional dynamics in their present families, and to *see* how those dynamics developed and were passed on through past generations. The goal is *not to blame*. At first, it is almost impossible for us not to blame someone for this mess that we're in. Only later can we detach from our parents and grandparents enough to say, "What went on with them was not healthy. I can choose to live another way even if they don't so choose."

As Bill and Anita explored their family backgrounds with their therapists and in their support groups, the following generational picture emerged.

There were no *obvious* addictions in Bill's parents' marriage. Mom and Dad Hopkins were teetotalers, in fact, who had no addictions to any *chemical substances* at all. And at first, Bill described his childhood and his relationships with his parents as "just normal". But as his process of self-discovery continued, bits and pieces started to fall into place. Bill's dad was a hard-working "bring-home-the-bacon" kind of guy who ran his own auto mechanic shop in the small town where they lived. He spent a lot of time teaching Bill how to fix cars, and he seemed to be actively involved in raising Bill. But he was also an extreme perfectionist. Their garage was always spotless. Their house was always quiet. Everything was always under complete control, and there was never a question about Dad wearing the pants in the family. He had quite a temper, too. He never carried a grudge, but he was painfully critical whenever Bill would make a mistake, make a mess in the garage when working on cars, or somehow not live up to his expectations for Bill.

Thus Bill grew up with a highly overdeveloped inner critic that was always telling him that if he didn't do it perfectly, then it wasn't worth doing at all.

Bill described his mother as "a saint." She was shy, retiring and very hardworking. She kept a spotless home and raised five children, of whom Bill was the oldest. She also received strong messages about perfection from her husband, and was emotionally distant from the children. Bill never remembers his parents hugging or kissing in front of the children, and in fact, doesn't remember anyone in the family being comfortable with appropriate touching.

Despite the perfectionism and domination of the family by his dad, Bill at first did not see the connection between that and his own problems. In going back another generation, the pieces started to fit more, though. His grandfather on his father's side was never diagnosed alcoholic, but it was a well-kept family secret that he had a pretty serious drinking problem.

Grandpa Hopkins led two lives. Outside of the home, he was generous, charming, humorous and well-liked by the community. Inside the home he was a tyrant who screamed and yelled when his wife asked for grocery money or extra money for school clothes for the children. He drank a lot at home, too, it turned out.

Grandma Hopkins was a quiet, compliant woman who tried to keep the peace by going along with whatever her husband demanded. They, too, showed no outward affection with each other.

On his mother's side, his grandparents' roles were just the opposite. His Grandpa Smith was a quiet, shy man, who always felt pretty worthless, who never really "made anything of himself," and who did what his wife told him to do.

Grandma Smith was domineering and controlling, and angry and bitter about her husband's perceived failure in life. She had a quick temper and was perfectionistic to an extreme. As the oldest child, Bill's mother identified strongly with her father and was kept in her place by her angry mother, and thus grew up not knowing how to be warm and nurturing.

As we so often do when dependencies are left untreated, Bill's mother married a man who had many of the negative traits of her mother believing that his strength and sense of goal-directedness would fill in her own lack of these. And what she first saw as strength, eventually emerged as all-out domination. The fact that he had "made something of himself" far overshadowed the fact that he had some clear problems in being intimate and supportive in a marriage.

And so the pieces began to fall into place for Bill. Patterns began to emerge that made sense. To avoid the confusion that you may have about this family so far, we have outlined Bill's family tree, in terms of the important personality dynamics, in Figure 7.1, using the diagram that Bill eventually put together for his own understanding.

The other piece of the puzzle that is missing, of course, is how Anita became entwined in this system. As is almost always the case, the spouse of the person who goes in for treatment or counseling rarely sees their own contribution to the problem because they have become so overly focused on their partner's problems that they can't see anything else. It is also common that their focus on their partner is an unconscious way to avoid looking at their own untreated dependencies. Remember paradoxical dependency?

At first Anita told herself, "Why, there's nothing for me to work on. When Bill finally stops acting out, all of our problems will vanish. I'm responsible. I'm the strong one in this marriage. Without me everything would have fallen apart long ago!"

Figure 7.1. Bill's Family

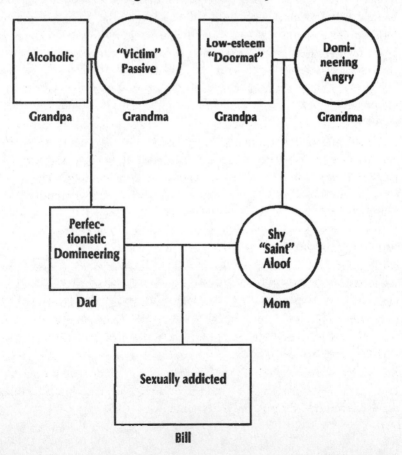

Fortunately for Anita and Bill, the treatment program Bill entered was aware of family dynamics and co-dependency, and they knew that it takes two to tango. Anita began to discover things about herself and her family that she had never examined before, and she found it to be just as painful and scary as Bill's discoveries about himself.

She knew all along that her mother had a tendency to rely on alcohol under stress, but she had never let it cross her mind that maybe her mother was alcoholic. Her mother had never passed out, had never gotten "sloppy drunk" in front of her, and had never seemed to have a problem.

And Anita had always seen her father as the ultimate "Dad." He was hardworking, responsible, cooked dinner when Anita's mom wasn't feeling well, played with the children on weekends, went to school plays and concerts, and was always easygoing and pleasant. What Anita didn't know was that Dad was very tired inside, and mildly depressed much of the time, really not the happy-go-lucky guy that he tried to be on the outside.

And it never bothered her that no one seemed to know anything about her grandparents on either side of her parents' marriage. All anyone seemed to know was that they were European, and that both of Anita's parents had come to America in their early teens, accompanied by aunts and uncles, or something.

As the oldest child in her family, Anita identified very strongly with her father and took on the role of the "good girl." When Mom was tired or "ill," Anita would help Dad do the cleaning and cooking. She would babysit the other children gladly, even when she was a teenager and could have been out with her friends, learning how to date and socialize. It didn't bother her when Mom was cranky and irritable, because like Dad, "she understood." Mom wasn't feeling well.

So from a very early age, Anita became a little parent, giving up her own childhood to take care of domestic chores, do well in school and stand *beside* Dad as one of the "adults" in the family. This became her set-up and her steel trap. With the trap securely set over years and years of growing up in her family, Anita was ready to go out into the world and get into her own dysfunctional relationship.

Figure 7.2. Bill and Anita

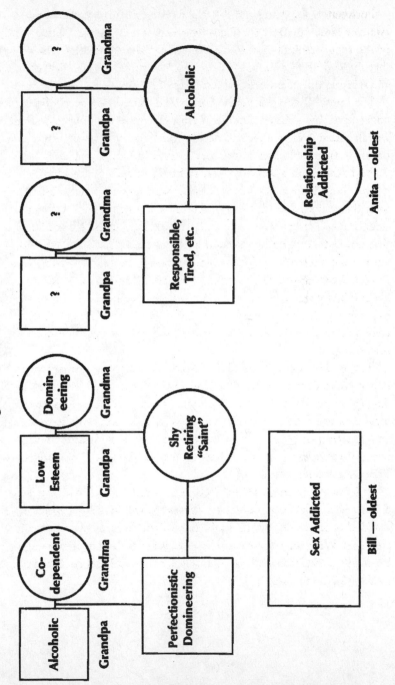

In Figure 7.2, we have reproduced Anita's family diagram that grew out of months of her own self-exploration, anguish and pain. We have set her family next to Bill's so that the entire system can be viewed at one time. You may want to study this system for awhile. It is a very common one.

What Bill and Anita discovered in their long journey together makes so much sense to them now, after many years of struggle, that it is hard for them to remember that nothing made sense to them before. The patterns, the early messages, the subtle conditioning, the unintentional pain that they grew to know, all fit into a coherent scheme now. They have moved beyond denial, through anger and blame, and on into peaceful acceptance of what *was*. They are living now, not in desperation and in the emptiness of not knowing what or why, but in the confidence and serenity of coming to terms with what was, and in the freedom that comes with putting what was to *rest.* And if this sounds too good to be true, believe us, it isn't.

What is difficult to convey is the process that people like Anita and Bill go through to reach this point of wholeness. The patterns that they unraveled and put back together were patterns of emotional denial going back many generations. They were patterns of fear of closeness with people, of fear of being vulnerable, of addictive patterns large and small, of individual selves trying to survive, of little children trying to fit into families and a larger world outside that weren't always functional.

8

When Families
Get Off Course

What are some of the things that can go wrong as we grow up? What are some of the dysfunctional patterns that happen in families and make us vulnerable to addictive patterns of living? Just as a flower needs sunlight, water and soil to grow up healthy and bloom, children need certain things from their families to emerge as adults who have a healthy sense of *interdependence*. We know of no families that provide all of these things perfectly, but we know of many families in which enough of these things were not provided so that the children growing up in these families entered adulthood with serious dependencies.

In a healthy family, children's needs for security, warmth, nurturance and guidance are met most of the time. These children enter adulthood with a sense of security and trust that is *inside of themselves*. In dysfunctional families, these needs are not met enough or at all, and these children enter adulthood with a sense of incompleteness, mistrust and fear *inside* of themselves, along with a strong need for some kind of security *outside* of themselves. As adults who grew up in troubled families, we constantly seek to fill up the empty parts inside of us that were never met while we were growing up, and

71

it is the *external* search for our unmet needs that leads us into addictive lifestyles. In our many talks around the country we have found the following analogy to be most helpful:

Figure 8.1. The Cup

Imagine yourself to be a cup (see Figure 8.1) which at birth is empty. Your goal as you grow up is to get the cup filled. In other words, you have certain needs that must be met. In a healthy family you get your cup filled almost to the top, and so when you go out into the world, you make friends and/or fall in love with others whose cups are full. If you came from a dysfunctional family, your cup didn't get filled. In extreme cases, it may only be

1/8th full when you become an adult. *So when you go out into the world, you make friends and/or fall in love with others whose cups are about 1/8th full.* And to maintain the illusion that your cup is full, you rely on outside agents such as addictive relationships, chemicals, work, television, etc.

It is our belief that our symptoms come from not having our cups filled while we were growing up in our families. Instead of learning healthy ways to live and grow, we learned some unhealthy ways to be, because of certain things that were going on in our families. It is these things that set our traps for us.

In looking at the emotional health or lack of health in a family system, we suspect that families are probably normally distributed just like most other traits in nature and in psychology specifically (see Figure 8.2).

The majority of us, approximately 2/3, fall in the average range, with an average amount of health and an average amount of dysfunction. This means that the majority of us have our cups filled up partially, but by no means fully. This also means that the majority of us have some clear-cut dysfunction to work on, and some clear-cut addictive or other symptoms that plague us.

Notice that only a very small percentage of us are in the extremely healthy range. And even for extremely healthy people, problems exist like they do for the rest of us. The difference in these families is that the problems are handled in healthy ways. Conflicts get resolved. Children grow up and leave home, which still pulls at parents' heartstrings. People still inherit genetic predispositions for chemical dependency, obesity, depression, and the like. But they handle their genetic endowment differently than the rest of us.

At the other extreme are families that are extremely unhealthy, where there is a lot of mental illness, repeated incest and battering, and child death. In the following pages we will describe some of the characteristics of dysfunctional families that we and others have written about in the past (Black, 1981; Fossum & Mason, 1986; Subby & Friel, 1985). We also refer the reader to the works of internationally known psychoanalyst Alice Miller, especially her book entitled *For Your Own Good* (Miller, 1983), in which she coins the term "Poisonous Pedagogy" to describe the methods of physical and emotional abuse that parents use to "guide" and "mold" their children. She makes a compelling and scholarly argument for the family-of-origin roots of our adult symptoms, including descriptions of the more covert types of abuse that nearly all of us have experienced.

Figure 8.2. Health/Dysfunction Continuum

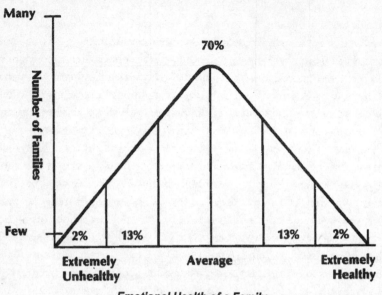

Emotional Health of a Family

Normal curve demonstrating that roughly two-thirds of the population at large falls within the average range of the health/dysfunction continuum.

On our continuum from extremely healthy to extremely unhealthy families, you will find some or all of these characteristics listed below, depending on how functional or dysfunctional a family is. Some families have few if any of them, and some families have all of them.

1. Physical, emotional or sexual abuse/neglect and vicarious abuse
2. Perfectionism
3. Rigid rules, lifestyle and/or belief systems
4. The "No Talk Rule"/Keeping "The Family Secrets"
5. Inability to identify and/or express feelings
6. Triangulation (a communication pattern using one person as intermediary)
7. Double messages/double binds
8. Inability to play, have fun and be spontaneous

9. High tolerance for inappropriate behavior/pain

10. Enmeshment

As you process them in more depth, remember that the *degree* of overall dysfunction is what matters, and that this "degree" depends not just on how many of these traits exist in a family, but also how *often* they occur. We know of no one who doesn't have little rituals or rigidities in his life. It is when these rigidities begin to interfere with healthy intimacy, with family members' feelings of wholeness and dignity, that problems begin to crop up.

Frank, our California engineer, grew up with "everything" any child could ever want—a father who was a doctor, a mother who was active in the community, a good education, athletic ability, good looks, vacations at the lake and money—yet his own marriage and life were thrust into chaos because he never really learned how to *feel* and *be*. He became so overly competent at "doing" that he never had the time or the family guidance to learn how to be in "non-doing relationship" with other people.

In our busy world it's such a simple thing to overlook, and there are no evil bogeymen to blame. It happens much too often, and the end result is just plain sad. The happy news is that it doesn't have to stay that way. We aren't bears. We have bigger brains to figure out those traps sooner or later, and it's *never* too late to start looking at those traps as the traps that they are.

As you read through our descriptions of these traps, it is absolutely normal and "okay" to: (1) say to yourself, "that never happened in my family,"(2) feel confused, (3) get really mad at us or your family, (4) wonder, (5) question, (6) doubt, (7) feel sad, (8) cry, (9) want to talk to someone about it, or (10) be bored.

Physical, Emotional or Sexual Abuse and Neglect/Vicarious Abuse

As recently as 1975, one psychiatric textbook reported that child sexual abuse occurs in only one family in a million (Kohn, 1987). This simply underscores the tremendous denial and fear on the part of educated professionals regarding the nature of the human animal.

The facts tell a different story. As many as one in six people in this country were sexually abused as children. And in one recent study it was discovered that roughly 30% of all women and 15% of all men were sexually abused by physical contact, ranging from fondling to intercourse, while they were still children. When noncontact forms of sexual abuse are included, the figure increases to around 50% for women (Kohn, 1987).

Sexual abuse occurs most frequently when children are between the ages of 9 and 12, but it also occurs with regularity in infancy, which makes it extremely difficult for a recovering person to ever identify and deal with it.

While we basically agree with the work of Lloyd de Mause (1974), who makes a good case for the general improvement of the lot of children from ancient to present day times, the statistics on abuse and neglect in this country are still staggering. A lot of children get *damaged* in this country by *very overt* means such as beating, battering, severe neglect and sexual abuse. And this is just the tip of the iceberg. The more *covert* and *subtle* forms of abuse and neglect are only recently being studied with any precision. Those of us in the psychotherapy field see it all the time.

A great deal of what we write about in this book comes under the category of abuse. At the end of this section we offer a list of the most common types of abuse that we see. We offer the following as food for thought.

Children need to be punished to grow straight and tall, right? Perhaps. But do your children cower in fear when you show the least bit of anger? Are they fearful? Do they seem unwilling to play and have fun? Are they unusually angry and aggressive? Do they pick on the younger children in the family unmercifully? Are they moody, negative and "difficult"? If you were punished too much or too severely as a child yourself, you won't be able to tell the difference between appropriate punishment and what we now call abuse. It's not your fault that you can't tell the difference. But you won't be able to tell the difference, no matter whose fault it was.

Letting children into your marital arguments and trying to get your emotional needs met by your children is a form of emotional abuse called covert incest by many professionals including Woititz (1985). Criticizing your shy child for being too shy is emotional abuse.

Screaming at your child because you're exhausted or have a hangover is emotional abuse. Not being there enough for your child is emotional abuse, as is hovering over your child and never letting him fall down, make mistakes on his own and recover on his own where appropriate for his age.

Many of us are quick to say, "Oh, I was lucky. My parents *never* fought when I was a kid. Billy's dad was always drunk and they were always fighting." That may be true. But finding the worst example of abuse in someone else's life for comparison is one of the best ways to maintain our own denial about our own families. The truth is we know of few families that don't have *some* of these problems. What were the problems in *your* family? Forget Billy's family. Billy has to deal with that. Deal with your own.

If you are witness to the abuse of anyone else, then you are also a victim of abuse. If you observe your little sister or big brother being hurt by Mom or Dad, it does emotional violence to you, too. You may feel guilty that you were treated "better." You may feel powerful in unhealthy ways because you were treated "better," which will then make it hard for you to have an equal relationship with another person. You may feel frightened that if you don't hold your breath and toe the mark, you will become the next victim of family violence. Seeing someone else be abused is called vicarious abuse, and it is just as painful, hurtful, and harmful as other kinds of abuse. Below is our list.

Emotional Abuse

Double binds (all choices given the child are negative ones)

Projection and transfer of blame onto the child

Alterations of the child's reality (intellectual abuse), e.g., "Dad's not drunk, he's just tired"

Overprotecting, smothering, excusing, blaming others for the child's problem

Fostering low self-esteem

Double messages: "Of course, I love you, dear," (as Mom tenses up and grits her teeth)

Not talking about the abuse at all

Emotional Neglect

Failure to nurture, care for or love the child

Failure to provide structure or set limits

Not listening to, hearing or believing the child

Expecting the child to provide emotional nurturing to the parents, to make the parent feel good

Not being emotionally present due to mental illness, chemical dependency, depression, or compulsivity

Failure to encourage education or intellectual development

Physical Neglect

Lack of food, clothes, shelter

Leaving the child alone in age-inappropriate ways

Leaving a child who is too young in charge of others

Failure to provide medical care

Allowing or encouraging the use of drugs, alcohol

Failure to protect the child from the abuse of others, including spouse

Verbal Abuse

Excessive guilting, blaming, shaming

Name-calling, put-downs, comparisons

Teasing, making fun of, laughing at, belittling

Nagging, haranguing, screaming, verbal assault

Physical Abuse

Slapping, shaking, scratching, squeezing, hitting, beating with boards, sticks, belts, kitchen utensils, yardsticks, electric cords, shovels, hoses

Throwing, pushing, shoving, slamming against walls or objects

Burning, scalding, freezing

Forcing of food or water, starving

Having to watch others be physically abused

Overworking

Sexual Abuse/Neglect

Fondling, touching

Innuendos, jokes, comments, looking, leering

Exposing self to, masturbating in front of

Mutual masturbation

Oral sex, anal sex, intercourse

Penetration with fingers or objects

Stripping and sexual punishments/enemas

Pornography—taking pictures or forcing the child to watch

Forcing children to have sex with each other

Enforced sexual activity with animals

Watching others have sex or be abused

Sexual "games"

Sexual "torture"—burning, etc.

Not teaching children about sex—allowing sexual naivete

Not talking about puberty, menstruation, nocturnal emissions, etc.

Vicarious Abuse

A special case of abuse, in which the victim is part of a family or other system in which *someone else* is abused in some way. This type of abuse can be just as damaging as actually being the recipient of the other types of abuse listed above.

Perfectionism

Perfectionism is common and can be one of the most easily denied and excused flaws in any family. It is also easily misunderstood. Perfectionism includes having unrealistic expectations for self or others, and it is conveyed not only by obvious criticism and belittling, but also by more subtle means, like a well-timed frown, a downturned glance, a quizzical look coupled with a pregnant pause, or a smirk disguised as a lack of understanding.

"You were embarrassed at that party?" Dad asks innocently, with an edge of contempt at your vulnerability in his voice. "What were you embarrassed for?" he adds. What a trap! He obviously doesn't approve of your *feeling* embarrassed, but he also wants to know why you were embarrassed. No matter what you say now, you're in trouble and the message is strong and clear no matter what. "We don't get embarrassed in our family." You failed. You didn't meet the expectation.

Or take Bill for another example. When he worked on cars with his father, he learned a tremendous amount about automobile engines. By the age of 13 he could tear an engine apart and put it back together again. Yet at the end of every weekend of working on cars, he was always left with a knot in his stomach and a feeling of worthlessness in his heart because of his father's critical perfectionism about keeping the garage "perfect." Instead of telling

Bill's mother, "Boy, Bill sure did a great job on that car today!" which would have been true, he more often than not would say, "Well, *someday* he'll learn how to be a real mechanic, when he learns to keep the damned garage clean!"

Perfectionism, in our opinion, is an unhappy person's way to hang onto the illusion that his life is under control. Perfectionism grows out of un-happiness and is the breeding ground for constant criticism. And constant criticism is the surest way to leave a child with a deep sense of worthless-ness and shame. Think of some of the perfectionistic, critical statements that you received from *your* parents or teachers or boss, or of the ones that you give to your own children.

"Why did you spill your milk, Susie? Can't you do anything right?"

"Do you have to wear *that* tie?"

"I wish you could be like your big brother. *He* always . . ."

"It's fine that you got three A's and a B, but what's this C for?"

"Why do you want to be an *art* major? You won't make any money doing that."

"What did you do *that* for?"

"You don't think of anyone except yourself."

"That's *not* the way the dishes are supposed to go in the dishwasher!"

"Look at you, you're a mess!"

"Can't you say *anything* that makes sense?"

The list goes on and on, but we hope the point is made. Constant criti-cism and perfectionism affects *everyone* in the family, including the one who is doing the criticizing. It produces not only shame, but eventually distances us from the people who are doing the criticizing. It makes us unhappy. It leaves a cloud hanging in the air over everything we feel and do and say.

People who grow up in critical families will eventually *internalize* all of those messages so that when they enter adulthood, they will unconsciously do the same thing to themselves. A little voice inside of them will always be saying, "This isn't good enough. You're not doing it right. There's something *wrong* with you." That's right. There's something wrong with you. I spill the milk and therefore there's something wrong with *me? With my very being? With my identity?* Does that make sense? It doesn't have to make sense, but it's exactly what happens. And it's very sad that it does. There is no room for mistakes.

Rigid Rules, Lifestyle And/Or Belief Systems

There is only one right way to be. There is only one right way to do it. I must be in control at all times or my life will topple. An awful lot of compulsive behavior and obsessive thinking comes under this heading. It is one thing to have clear beliefs and values. It is another to be a slave to those beliefs, and to force those beliefs onto someone else.

Family rituals are important. *Compulsive* family rituals are destructive. Is American government the only one that works? Is it the only one that allows individual dignity? Is your church or religion the *only* one that can meet a person's need for spirituality? Are your political beliefs the *only* ones that are right? Must all children go directly to college after high school in order to make a success of their lives? Must boys *not* cry? Must girls become mothers to be fulfilled?

It doesn't matter that we're all tired and crabby. We said we were going to drive until we got to Florida today, and by God, that's what we're going to do. No matter that Mom isn't feeling well and needs to sleep. We need to get the house clean, and that's what we're going to do.

Compulsive, rigid rituals rob life of its spontaneity. The fun, the surprises in life, the unpredictability and the magic in life are viewed as dangerous and threatening. Joy is replaced by routine. Happiness is replaced by a dull plodding lifestyle that is neat and tidy, but empty and lonely. Those of us who grow up in rigid families find the normal confusion of interpersonal relationships, the ups and downs of friendship and the normal unpredictability of changing social networks to be more than we can bear. As adults, we seek out rigid, controlled relationships and social systems where the rules of life are spelled out in black and white. Unfortunately, life doesn't always work that way. And when life takes one of its unpredictable little turns, we are left feeling scared, cheated and manipulated, with no emotional tools for handling the uncontrollable. Part of living a full, happy life is being able to let go of the uncontrollable. Growing up in rigid, compulsive families does not prepare us at all for letting go.

The "No Talk Rule"/
Keeping "The Family Secrets"

Do you remember the old saying, "Don't air your dirty laundry in public"? Somewhere along the line this call for tact and discretion has become the battle cry of dysfunctional families. Granted, it probably does not make much sense to take out a full-page ad in your local newspaper announcing that Uncle Joe is an alcoholic. But have we gone overboard in the other direction?

In dysfunctional families, this rule means "Don't yell for help when you're about to drown." It means little children must go to school every day, smiles on their faces and knots in their stomachs, because they have been up half the night listening to their parents have a bloody battle over money, or alcohol, or in-laws. It means those same children dare not try to share their pain with a friend or a school counselor because if they do, they will be emotionally or physically beaten or shamed for sharing "family secrets" outside the family. Above all, it means that *we will grow up to believe that we must handle all of our problems by ourselves, alone, in isolation.*

"Don't you be talking about our problems with Mrs. Smith."

"I don't want to talk about it."

"We don't talk about those things in this family."

We all know the feeling. Something is upsetting us at home. We wish we could share it with someone to get a new perspective on things. But a little voice inside of us says, "If you let them know what's inside, they'll think you're crazy!" Or maybe it's, "They won't believe you anyway, or they won't understand or . . ." This rule is especially dangerous and destructive because it keeps family systems completely closed.

Remember Sandy's mother? She tried talking with a friend whose husband was in A.A., and her own husband threatened her so severely that she never spoke to her friend again. This kind of rule, in its extreme, is the worst form of tyranny. In milder forms, it leaves children with the belief that what is inside of them is bad unless it fits the family rules for what is and is not appropriate to talk about.

Menstruation? "It just happens. Don't talk about it." Anger? "We don't get angry at each other in this family." And so we are left feeling that a big chunk of our insides is *bad.* "If we don't talk about it, it will go away," we tell ourselves; but it never does.

Tina and Frank didn't talk about what was truly inside of them, until one day what was inside of Tina burst forth with such explosive force that she thought she was literally going insane. As noted psychotherapist Carl Rogers (1973) says, any *persistent* feeling should be expressed in a relationship, even if it seems trivial. If not, the resentment that builds eventually reaches destructive force and then we really have a mess on our hands. With the "No Talk Rule," these things never get expressed.

Within dysfunctional families, each family member will argue that they do share their problems—with someone else in the family. If the system is dysfunctional, then sharing the problems *only* with those in the system will do nothing but feed the sickness.

Dysfunction feeds on dysfunction. We become so mired in our own family problems that no one *within* the family has any vision whatsoever. It is like the blind leading the blind or the helpless helping the helpless, which in the long run never helps. Constructive change never happens in these systems until someone breaks out of the system. Very often this someone will be an alcoholic who kills someone while driving drunk, or a teenager who gets caught selling drugs, or a husband or wife who gets caught having an affair. Fresh air cannot get into these systems until something cracks this powerful wall of "Don't talk."

Inability to Identify or Express Feelings

This is a by-product of the "No Talk Rule" and of criticism and control within a family.

"Good children don't hate their brothers or sisters," we hear. And so when we feel angry at our sibling, we don't know what to do with it. The anger gets buried beneath a set of rules. Eventually a lot of other feelings get buried along with the anger. Feelings of sadness, hurt, fear and shame. As adults, we walk around with a mask on, behaving in ways and expressing feelings which we *think* are appropriate, which we *think* will lead to happiness. Instead, what happens is that we learn to deny who we are, we deny what we feel and we deny the reality around us. This perhaps is the ultimate error we make as we continually step into our own traps.

We don't learn from experience because it is too painful to admit our true feelings surrounding that experience.

"Oh, yes, I just stepped in a bear trap. Well, not all bear traps are bad, you know. I mean, without bear traps, where would we be? We wouldn't have safe parks, we wouldn't have bear-skin rugs." With our foot bloody and our ankle shattered, we say, "No, it doesn't hurt that much. Those things happen."

If this sounds far-fetched, think of what we say when we are in a relationship where we aren't getting our needs met.

"She stood me up for the fifth time in a row. Oh, well, I understand. She had to work late. She needed her time out with the girls. She . . ." To admit our true feelings in these situations would mean that we would have to admit a painful reality, that a bear trap has shattered our ankle and it hurts like hell, or that "she" is not good for us and doesn't respect us.

To admit that I feel lonely in my family would mean that there is something *wrong*. Because I am in a closed family system with a "No Talk Rule," there is no way for me to know if it is *me* who is wrong or my family who is wrong. Even if I am clever enough to realize that there is something wrong with my family system, I am part of that family system, whether consciously or unconsciously so, and therefore there must be something wrong with me, too. So it is much easier to just say, "I am wrong," or "I am bad," or "I am dirty," or "I am crazy." From there, it is a simple hop, skip and a jump to say, "I don't want to feel this at all. I'll just pretend it doesn't hurt and then maybe it will all go away."

We deny our *feelings*, which *are* our *reality*. Then we deny the objective reality around us (Dad doesn't get angry very often, really). And then we build a tidy shell around us so that on the outside we're looking *great* and on the inside we're suffocating. We humans are extremely clever, not like bears at all.

Triangulation

This refers to communication patterns within a family. Families who do this use one family member as a messenger or go-between, rather than speaking directly to the person with whom they want to communicate.

For example, Mom and Dad just had a fight. Dad thinks that he'll be able to get to Mom if he works through 10-year-old Bobby, so he says, "Bobby, will you go ask your mother if she's still mad at me? Tell her I really didn't mean what I said, and ask her if she wants to go to dinner with us." Being a good little trooper, Bobby does what he is asked. Mom says, "Bobby, you tell your father I wouldn't go to dinner with him if he was the last person on earth. And then you get upstairs and clean your room like I told you to do an hour ago."

Bobby was trying to be a good boy. He was trying to help get Mom and Dad back together, but he wound up with Mom taking out her anger toward Dad on him, and he was left feeling that part of their marital problem was his. He had failed in his mission. He had let down Dad. He had made a mess of things. Or so Bobby felt. How Bobby felt is all that matters. When triangulation becomes a regular fixture in a family system, communication becomes blurred, people become enmeshed in problems that are not theirs, and children, especially, become pawns in their parents' power struggles. And when you are made a pawn in someone else's game long enough, you become just a pawn to yourself, too. You become an object. You take on other people's feelings and guilts and sense of worthlessness.

Children who grow up with lots of triangulation going on at home between them and adults, and between adults and other adults, come to feel and believe that this is "normal," and so they repeat the pattern in their own adult lives. Because it feels "normal," they also gravitate to other adults who communicate this way.

In fact, when they encounter an adult who does not communicate this way, they think something is wrong. Thus, they shy away from people who communicate in healthy ways, and in so doing, manage to recreate the dysfunctional system they grew up in. This is true of all dysfunctional family patterns, this one included.

Double Messages/Double Binds

Tommy runs up to Dad when he gets home from work and asks, "Do you love me, Dad?"

"Sure, son," says Dad, as he buries his head in the newspaper, eats dinner, turns on the television set, sits there for three hours and then goes to bed.

Betsy runs up to Mom at bedtime, throws her arms around Mom and says, "I love you." Mom's back stiffens and her body gets tense because no one ever hugged in her family when she was growing up, "I love you, too, honey." Because Mom's double reaction was so subtle, Betsy doesn't appear to notice, but she does unconsciously.

Double messages are of the kind, "I love you/go away." "I need you/I don't need you." "We are proud of you/We are ashamed of you." "Sure, we like you/why can't you be more like your brother?" More often than not, these double messages are extremely subtle; and the more subtle they are, the harder it is to identify that they were ever there in the first place.

In one family that we worked with, Mom and Dad were always talking about how democratic they were and how hard they tried to treat each child equally. What they couldn't see because they had such a closed family system was that they were really doing just the opposite of what they said they were doing. Oldest brother was the "star." Middle sister was a quiet, shy girl who earned good grades in school but who had a heck of a time connecting with anyone else in the family or outside of it. And little brother, who was "the problem," was acting out in school and causing trouble at home. Oldest brother sat next to Dad, who appeared to wield most of the power in the family. Mom and Dad spoke in glowing terms about all of his accomplishments. Middle sister sat off to the side a bit, and Mom and Dad talked less enthusiastically about her. She was "the quiet one," they said. Little brother was more or less bouncing off the walls of our office, and everyone else spoke with humor and a touch of condescension about him. "He's the charmer in the family," they all chimed in, "but he's trouble, too," they laughed. "We're proud of our parenting skills," said Dad. "We treat each one just the same."

What really happened in this family is that oldest brother had been treated all along just like Dad. He had all the power and all the glory. Middle sister was treated just like Mom. She was quiet, shy and had no power at all. Little brother was treated like a toy, and wound up acting out all of the real dysfunction in the family and all of the real tension in the family that was being suppressed by Dad's unfair balance of power. The double message here, of course, is "We treat you all the same. We treat none of you the same."

It is true that no two children will be alike in any given family, and that each child will develop his or her own personality, as well they should. But it is dysfunctional when one child gathers up all of the power and attention in a family, or when one spouse in a partnership has all of the power. In this family, the notion of equality was a pipedream perpetrated by an authoritarian husband and father, and a mother who went along with it.

Inability to Play and Have Fun

This is one of the key characteristics of adult children of dysfunctional families. Many of us who became alcoholic, for example, are often seen as too "fun-loving and irresponsible," but the fact is that when we grow up in compulsive or addictive families the world is a very serious place to be. We are always on the edge of burnout. We are always trying to prove our worth by what we do, rather than accepting simply who we are.

Even Frank had a problem in this area. He "worked hard and played hard," but the play that he engaged in was highly structured and competitive. To be able to play means to be able to "let go." To be able to let go means to be able to trust, to be able to trust that we are okay even if we make a fool of ourselves now and then. It's pretty tough to truly play and not risk making a fool of ourselves.

Spontaneous laughter and humor is almost difficult for those children who, like Anita, took on the role of "the little parent" while growing up. Or who, like Sandy, used so much energy to appear "respectable" while at school, despite the horrible violence and chaos that was going on at home. In healthy families we can truly play and feel safe. We know that if things get out of hand, someone will get us back on course firmly but gently. In unhealthy families, play begins in a healthy way, but almost always ends up with someone getting damaged physically or emotionally. Nobody knows when to quit. Enough is never enough. Humor is used to hurt as often as it is used in Fun. "Letting go" escalates into chaos. Boundaries and limits are nonexistent. "Let's 'play' football" turns into "Let's prove who's better than everyone else." "Let's 'wrestle'" turns into "Let's hurt someone." "It's okay to flirt," turns into "I want to have an affair."

Again, as with other issues already discussed, the issue of play and spontaneity becomes one of extremes in dysfunctional families. It's either nothing at all, with everyone beinng deadly serious and morose, or total chaos and damage. As trite as it may sound, finding that middle path is the hardest accomplishment for an adult who grew up in an unhealthy family.

High Tolerance For
Inappropriate Behavior/Pain

This tells you how we become saints and martyrs as children, and how we then go out into the adult world and try to remain saints and martyrs. It comes from learning to deny our feelings when we are little, to protect ourselves from boundary violations and emotional or physical abuse. It comes from seeing one or both of our parents repeatedly refuse to take care of their own needs. It comes from religious or cultural rules that say others must always come first. It comes from watching self-destructive patterns of living in our parents who work too much, drink too much, take care of others too much, eat too much, yell too much, lie too much, jog too much and even play too much.

Through years and years of putting everyone else first and years of self-denial and denial of feelings, we come to pride ourselves in just how much we can put up with before we say "Ouch!"

"Doesn't it bother you that your mother is always so critical of you?" a healthy friend asks you. "Well, no," you say with hesitation, "she's had such a hard life and all. I understand why she does it." It's fine that you understand why she does it. But is it healthy for you to subject yourself to such abuse, day in and day out? What does that do to a person over the years? It's quite simple, really. *It teaches us to discount ourselves and to abuse ourselves.*

In many families, it's not only tolerance for inappropriate behavior that we learn. We also learn to put up with a lot of physical pain. A friend of ours had chronic ear infections when he was a little child, but his family was in such chaos that he rarely got to a doctor to have it treated. Dad was a particularly "macho" guy, and most of the time he would say, "Oh, come on now, Billy. It isn't that bad. Tough it out, boy." Mom was more sympathetic, but she was under such stress all the time that she simply couldn't get around to getting it taken care of properly. She spent most of her time fighting with Dad about "intimacy," as she called it.

So Billy learned to put up with a lot of pain: and slowly came to take pride in that "strength" he had. A lot of people were impressed with his pain tolerance as he gew into physical adulthood, as a matter of fact. It wasn't until Bill died of cancer at the age of 36 that anyone thought it was unhealthy.

You see, Bill had had painful symptoms for 18 months before he decided to consult with his doctor, and by then it was way too late. He died three months later.

As adults who have learned to tolerate lots of inappropriate behavior from others, we find ourselves replaying our childhoods in our current relationships. We get in abusive or manipulative relationships where our partners lie to us repeatedly, or hurt us physically, or criticize us unmercifully, and we just stay with that person. We make lots of excuses for their behavior. We pride ourselves in how tolerant and patient we are. We begin to believe that we are better than everyone else, because the only people we let into our lives are abusive people.

The popular saying, "Life's A Bitch And Then You Die," becomes our credo. We pray a lot, but we don't do anything to get out of the destructive relationship. We try to reform the other person, always hoping that today will be the day that she or he will change. But change rarely happens by itself.

What would someone with a full cup do when faced with an abusive or manipulative relationship? Our nine-year-old son said it best. We took him and our two daughters to see the film version of *The Color Purple* when it was first released. As we discussed the film in the kitchen that evening, David stood silent for a moment, and then thoughtfully asked, "Why didn't she just leave?" That, of course, is what someone with a full cup would do. They'd simply leave.

Enmeshment

Enmeshment is a term from family systems theory and is actually a problem in boundary definition. It is such a commonly used term nowadays that we also feel it deserves discussion on its own.

Put simply, enmeshment is a tangled mess. When people are enmeshed with each other, it is nearly impossible for them to see where their identities end and someone else's identity begins. My problems become your problems and your problems become my problems. I blame you for my unhappiness and you blame me for yours. I can't make a move without you knowing it and/or commenting on it, and vice versa.

In an enmeshed family, everyone is "into" everyone else's business. You can't go to the bathroom in an enmeshed family without someone taking note of it. Triangulation runs rampant in enmeshed families. Everyone is running around like chickens with their heads cut off, going from one person to the next, "spreading the news," trying to fix everyone else's problems, telling them how to live their lives, and so on.

No one has an identity of their own. There is no separateness. There is no clarity of boundaries. There is a lot of emotional incest. No one takes responsibility for their own lives. No one is allowed to live in peace. No one is allowed to make their own mistakes and learn from them with dignity. Everyone is so tangled up with everyone else that when one family member gets depressed, eventually every family member gets depressed; or everyone becomes manic to compensate for it. When one person goes on the upswing, everyone else goes on the upswing; or they get moody and depressed.

It's as if we're all in a life raft together at the mercy of constantly changing seas. Up and down, back and forth we go, one big happy family, caught in an endless web of emotions and problems.

NOTE

As we said earlier, there are many ways to describe family traits that lead to unhappy adulthood. We hope that our categories give you the basic idea. Perhaps the most important thing to keep in mind is that you have to live in your own body with your own feelings and with your own family history.

While it is extremely important to share your experience with others, it is also extremely important to avoid the "one up, one down" syndrome. It may be true that your childhood was a disaster when compared with your friend's. But it is also true that just around the corner awaits someone whose life is a disaster when compared to yours. The paradox of all of this is that we need to share our lives with other people and we need to define ourselves as individuals, separate from other people. In the world of family history and emotional development, all people are not created equal. On the surface, at least, life is not fair. Take your own inventory. And let your friends take theirs.

Interlude

9

The Goose

Once upon a time in a far away land called Northern Minnesota, there was a family of geese who lived on a quiet little pond on the outskirts of a small town. Mr. Gander and Mrs. Goose and their three goslings spent a lot of time in the pond, and they enjoyed their neighbors, Mr. Beaver and Mr. and Mrs. Loon.

On sunny afternoons after the wind had died down, they would congregate near Mr. Beaver's house and talk about their families and their plans for the winter. Like all normal Minnesotans, the weather was always at the top of the list for conversation.

"Hot enough for you, Mrs. Goose?" asked Mr. Loon.

"Land sakes, yes!" replied Mrs. Goose, with a mock sigh of consternation in her voice.

"Well, I don't know," piped in Mr. Beaver. "I sort of like this weather."

Mr. Gander listened out of one ear as he gazed out over the pond and thought about what a wonderful life they had all made for themselves. His goslings were growing up faster than he had ever imagined, and he was thinking ahead to the trip south that they'd all be taking in a few months. He was even thinking beyond that, to the time when they could return to this pond again after the long, cold Minnesota winter was over. He loved this place.

While all this adult conversation was going on, the three goslings were out in the middle of the pond skimming across the top of the water, feet paddling fast as they tried to get themselves airborne for the first time. None of them were to accomplish it today, but they would soon enough. As they stopped to rest, the Littlest Gosling spoke to his brother and sister. "You know, I haven't been feeling so great the past few days. My stomach has been a little queasy, and my head hurts just a bit."

"Well," his sister replied, "you're probably just anxious about the big trip south this winter. After all, it is a long way from home."

"Yes," his brother added, "and you've been working awfully hard to learn how to fly. Why don't you just go over by Mom and Dad and take a breather."

The Littlest Gosling frowned. "I don't know. It just feels like something's wrong. I can't quite put my wingtip on it, but something tells me things aren't right."

"You Silly Goose!" his brother and sister echoed in unison.

The Littlest Gosling began swimming toward the spot on the edge of the pond where his parents were. Before he reached them, he veered off to the left into a small cove lined with cattails and water lilies. He noticed a peculiar odor and spotted two dead fish floating bellies up on the surface of the water. He wondered if there was something wrong with his pond; and he wondered if that was why he was feeling a little sick.

He paddled out of the cove and around to his parents, Mr. Beaver, and Mr. and Mrs. Loon.

"Mom, Dad," he began, "I think there's something wrong with this pond. I think there's something in it that's making me sick." He gazed up into their eyes, awaiting that glimmer of pride and recognition in their expressions that would say they were interested in his discovery.

Instead, Mrs. Goose snapped, "Oh, you Silly Goose! Whatever gave you that idea? Land sakes, son, you come up with the silliest notions sometimes."

Disappointed but still holding out hope, he looked toward his father. "Yes, son, you do come up with the oddest ideas sometimes."

"Silly Goose," clucked Mr. Beaver and the Loons in unison.

Well, that was just about all that the Littlest Gosling could bear. His feelings were hurt, but he wanted to be like a gander, so he simply held his head up high, turned around slowly, and said, "I suppose so." And then he swam away.

That evening his parents, brother and sister all had a good laugh over the Littlest Gosling's "discovery".

"Why, we've been coming back to this pond every spring for as long as I can remember," spouted Mr. Gander. "And no one has ever been sick a day in his life since we've been here," added Mrs. Goose.

"Alright, alright," shouted the Littlest Gosling, "enough is enough!"

Over the next few days everyone forgot about the incident, and things pretty much went back to normal.

About two weeks later the Littlest Gosling began to feel sick again, but he'd learned his lesson the first time, so he didn't even think about telling anyone in the pond about it.

At first he didn't know quite what to do. He went back to the small cove and saw some more dead fish and smelled that smell again. Then he took a tour of the rest of the pond and discovered some of the same things going on. A few dead fish here and there, a funny smell and a slight headache and queasy stomach that wouldn't seem to go away.

By now he was able to fly, and although he was feeling weak, he decided to break the rule that his parents had made for him and his brother and sister, and he flew up and over the edge of the pond and away. After gaining altitude, he noticed a big lake off in the distance with a large population of geese, ducks and loons, and so he headed toward it.

After a few minutes, he landed gracefully on the surface of the lake about 50 yards from a big gaggle of geese who were swimming about, enjoying the late afternoon sun. He was hesitant at first because his parents had told him not to leave his own pond, and because these geese were strangers. But they were very nice, and they invited him to come and join them in their conversation.

Soon after they began to talk, the Littlest Gosling told them what had been happening to him lately. As he talked, the Eldest Gander of the gaggle became very serious. The Littlest Gosling noticed that a frown swept across his face, and then suddenly the Eldest Gander began honking furiously.

"Where exactly do you live, son?" he asked the Littlest Gosling.

"A few minutes from here, as the goose flies," he answered. "In that pond behind that abandoned farm." The Eldest Gander honked even louder now.

"You must fly home and warn your family at once! And everyone else who lives there, too. That pond is poison! Believe me. We lived there once, too." His face grew sad. "I lost two of my goslings because of that pond."

The Littlest Gosling did not hesitate for an instant. He took to the air and flew directly to where his parents were swimming in the pond.

"Dad! Mom!" he shouted. "I know I'm not supposed to leave the pond, but I just had to get away. I was feeling so sick. And I was so curious. Anyway, I talked to some geese in a lake near here, and the Eldest Gander there said that the water in this pond is poison, and that he lost two goslings because of it. We need to get out of here right away!" he said excitedly.

Mr. Gander looked sternly at his son and said, "We told you never to leave this pond until we are all ready to fly south for the winter. You have broken our most important rule. We are very disappointed in you. Now go back to the nest and don't leave there until we tell you to!"

The Littlest Gosling was heartbroken and terrified. He didn't know what to do. He loved his family, and he wanted to be a good gosling, but he didn't want his family to die either. He began to return to the nest. When he was almost there, he suddenly turned, looked up into the sky, recalled the words of the Eldest Gander, and then flew off toward the big lake.

He had decided to live rather than to die but he was so deeply sad that he cried for the better part of four days. Members of the gaggle on the big lake would stop by to comfort him, and to tell him that he had made the right decision, but he still felt a deep pain inside. On several occasions, he almost got up and flew back to the pond, thinking that to die with his family would be better than to live with strangers. But each time, something deep inside of him told him to stay put.

And then something happened. Almost three weeks after he had left home, he saw a lone goose, or was it a gosling, winging its way toward the lake. His eyes were riveted on the bird. His heart leaped when he realized that it was his brother. His brother had started to feel sick, too. He had got in a huge fight with Mr. Gander but had finally decided to join the Littlest Gosling. Three days later, his sister joined them and a week after that, so did Mrs. Goose. Finally, one week later Mr. Gander, sick to his stomach and with a headache throbbing in his temples, joined the rest of the family on the big lake.

It took a lot of courage on their part, but once they were settled into their new home, Mr. and Mrs. Gander called a meeting of all the flocks.

As a hush settled over the lake, Mr. Gander put his wing around the Littlest Gosling and said, "This is my Littlest Gosling. For a while I thought he was a Bad Little Gosling. I thought he was a Selfish Little Gosling. I thought he was a Silly Goose. But he wasn't. We were the Silly Geese. And the Littlest Gosling saved our lives. We are proud of him."

A tear trickled down the beak of Mrs. Goose. It was a tear of pride and relief and gratitude. The Littlest Gosling's heart filled with warmth as every duck, loon, goose and gander on the big lake began honking their loudest honks and calling their loudest calls to celebrate his courage, wisdom and strength.

That winter they all flew south together and in the spring they returned to the big lake. They were pleased now to be a part of all the flocks safe in the knowledge that their water was pure, their friends were true and that their goslings would be able to grow up to be healthy and strong.

Part III

What Happens To Me?

"Some say that we are different people at different periods of our lives, changing not through effort of will, which is a brave affair, but in the easy course of nature every ten years or so . . . I think one remains the same person throughout, merely passing as it were in these lapses of time from one room to another, but all in the same house. If we unlock the rooms of the far past we can peer in and see ourselves, busily occupied in beginning to become you and me."

J. M. Barrie, from the Dedication to his first edition of **Peter Pan**

10

The Denial

"I don't need any help. I can overcome this myself."

"Marital problems? We don't have any marital problems. George has just been so tired lately from too much stress."

"But I'm not a . . ."

"We didn't have any alcoholism in *our* family. Well, Grandma liked her brandy now and then, but . . ."

Martin Short, one of the creative stars of NBC's *Saturday Night Live*, portrayed the epitome of defensiveness and denial in one of the characters that he developed for that show.

Recovering alcoholics have uproarious laughs when one of their fellows recalls acting seriously the way that Short acted in jest.

"I know that. Everybody knows that. It's so silly that you would think that I didn't know that. I'm not getting defensive. It's you who're getting defensive. I'm not defensive!"

Denial is one of the ways that we protect ourselves from a reality that is too painful for us to let into our conscious minds. It serves a healthy purpose as well as an unhealthy one, depending upon how we use it. When we suffer a catastrophic loss, it is appropriate for us to go into a state of denial for a while. It's as if a protective shield goes up, which we can later let down little by little as our egos are able to make sense out of the tragedy. This is what we do when someone close to us dies, when we lose a job, when our house burns to the ground or when we are informed that we have a terminal illness. As our psychic wounds begin to heal, we let more and more of the reality become real, until one day we are ready to go on with the rest of our lives.

In dysfunctional systems the catastrophe that hits us is a continuous one and denial becomes a way of life, rather than a protective measure to be used only in extreme circumstances. The pain of living in a dysfunctional system is akin to slow torture as opposed to dying an instantaneous death. Day-by-day, year-by-year, decade-by-decade, we crawl deeper and deeper into a shell of denial, defensiveness, isolation and emptiness that is fueled by our shame and embarrassment at the thought of anyone ever finding out what is really going on inside of us. That is the nature of dysfunctional systems—they are closed and implosive, ever more self-destructive. In that sense, they are just like malignant tumors in the body.

Denial is very tricky to spot sometimes, too. We know many people who have actually quit drinking or using cocaine entirely, and yet who are still in almost complete denial about their disease. We know of others who can clearly state that they are work addicted or drug addicted or relationship addicted, and yet continue to fuel and practice their addiction.

They say, "I'm not in denial. I know I'm an alcoholic. How can I be in denial?"

Well, take a look around you! Open your eyes! Look at the trail of destruction you continue to leave in your path. Look at the empty, desperate relationships. Look at the spouses and children and friends who are struggling painfully with the way that you treat them. They love you but they hate you. They want to be with you but they are terrified of you. They are becoming addicts of one sort or another themselves.

We Are All In Denial

We can buy a new house, have another child, move to a new city, switch from whiskey to beer or try any number of other pointless, useless tricks to "make things right," but until we admit that things are not the way we fantasize them, nothing gets better. And all of us in the addictive system do it, not just the one at whom we are all pointing our fingers.

Mom may be the "Identified Addict" who is hooked on Valium; but if you've been in the system for any length of time, you're some kind of an addict as well. Addiction breeds addiction. We make excuses for the self-destructive addictions of our loved ones because underneath it all, we are struggling with the same problems. It's simply a lot safer to point our fingers at someone else.

What's more, we learned our denial way back in childhood and brought it with us into adulthood, which is why we wound up with a cocaine addict or a sex addict or a TV junkie in the first place.

Part of the denial is that when we finally realize what has happened, we can't figure out how it happened. Look at a truly healthy woman, someone from that top 5% of the normal curve who really does have it all together. She dates a guy who seems to be on the ball. Because they're dating, he's on his good behavior. He has a cocaine problem, but she's one fine catch and so he doesn't use much around her. In fact, he probably uses less around her than anyone else. And we all know, though, cocaine addiction is about much more than using too much cocaine. It goes much deeper. It means that all kinds of other things are missing in our developmental picture. It means our cups are not very full. Think about it. Don't you think a truly healthy woman is going to spot something else wrong? Of course, she will.

It's elementary, my dear Watson. After a few dates she'll get a funny feeling when she's around him. She may not even be able to label it in words, but that won't matter. Being healthy, she will have learned long ago to trust her gut feelings about people. She'll notice that he may get uncomfortable in certain types of intimate conversations, or that his moods fluctuate a little more than she would like, or that there are certain parts of his life that he seems to have blocked out, or any number of other subtle cues that aren't so subtle to her.

If she's truly healthy, she probably won't back away from him right away, but she will keep the brakes on the relationship enough until her gut feeling tells her to go forward, because she's learned from her own past experiences. When she was younger, she may have rushed headlong into a relationship like this one and eventually been burned. She probably did it when she was still a teenager or in her early twenties. Being healthy, and having a pretty full emotional cup, she was able to get out because she wasn't desperate for love. Sure, it hurt for a while, but it wasn't the end of the world. And best of all, because she wasn't in a constant state of denial, she learned from her experiences. That's the saddest part of denial. It keeps us from ever learning from our mistakes.

And so she waits and watches. Sooner or later her friend's underlying dependency will be exposed. He will want to "catch" her. He will want to possess her. He will want to capture her now and for all time, to fill in that terrible void in himself that he has been filling up with cocaine. He will want to get married. He will want to spend more and more time with her. Or in punishment for her not giving him all that he wants when he wants it, he will pull away for no reason for periods of time. He will become "gamey," and the relationship for him will become like a chess match instead of a healthy, respectful interaction.

Eventually, he will make a big mistake. He'll pout or explode in a rage, or he'll go on a binge when he least expected it and she'll find out about it. With her gut feelings confirmed, she'll honestly and tactfully pull back. As she pulls back his symptoms of severe dependency will escalate. She'll pull back some more in healthy self-protection. Then it will be over. She'll breathe a sigh of relief. He'll mutter that she's a "bitch." She will have had her reality confirmed. He will return to his denial.

"At least I can use when I want to now," he'll say to himself. "She wasn't such a fine catch after all."

And the continuing darkness of denial will again envelope him. "The last time I talked to her, she said she thought I had a cocaine problem and that I should get some help for it. Humph! I've got a problem? She must be kidding. Everybody knows I don't have a problem. She's the one who has the problem. It's so funny that she should say I have a problem when it's so obvious to everybody that she's got the problem."

Martin Short, eat your heart out. Someone's trying to outdo you again, and he's doing a darned good job of it.

Many psychotherapists have a saying, "It's going to have to feel a lot worse before it feels better." Denial keeps us from ever feeling truly better.

It's like a friend of ours who had a mild infection under her fingernail. The tip of her finger began to swell up until it was pretty painful. She finally consulted her physician, who immediately became concerned, injected her finger with novacaine, and proceeded to rip off her fingernail and dig out the underlying infection. Did that ever hurt! Strangely enough, a few days later, the pain went away. Within a few weeks, her finger was as good as new.

Denial is just like that. It's like the tissue encasing a boil, protecting the rest of the body from the infection. And just like with boils, we sometimes can't heal ourselves.

In the case of the denial surrounding our addictions, this is almost universally true. The casing of psychological "tissue" gets thicker and thicker, the boil gets bigger and bigger and we experience more pain. The more pain we feel, the thicker the denial gets. We repeat the same mistakes over and over. The boil gets bigger and bigger. Without help, it finally bursts, and then we have a real mess on our hands. With addictions, this mess isn't just a little blood and pus. It's divorce, abuse, depression or death. Long-term denial simply doesn't do anybody any good. Ever.

11

The Feelings

All Of Our Symptoms Are Feeling Diseases.
If you remember nothing else from reading this book, please remember that. Our symptoms are unhealthy mechanisms that we use to keep from feeling our feelings. They smother, hide, distort and mix up our feelings. They turn fear and sadness into rage. They create depression from anger, fear from loneliness. In many cases, they cause a unique distortion in which the rich, full range of normal human emotions is channeled into one or two overpowering feelings. In this way, loneliness, sadness, fear, shame and rejection all get thrown into the pot together and get expressed as anger.

The anger is then manifested as bitterness, unhappiness with one's life or with the people in one's life. It takes the form of constant criticism, constant dissatisfaction, perfectionism, belligerence, argumentativeness, combativeness and other types of emotional abuse.

In this same way, feelings of tenderness, softness, warmth, safety, closeness and sensuality all get thrown into one pot and get expressed as lust, which is why the spouses of all kinds of addicts say that their sex is great sometimes, but that they feel lonely and empty in the relationship nonetheless. There is nothing wrong per se with anger or lust.

What we are stating is that when these are the only feelings that we feel, then there is something wrong. Human beings feel more than just these two.

As many physicians already know too well, the toll of this emotional blunting and distortion is more than just troubled relationships. A constantly hurried and angry style of life leads to increased risk of heart disease and heart attack. A stressful, other-focused lifestyle leads to any number of stress-related disorders from hypertension and headache to gastric problems, fatigue and chronic depression. These are all "feelings" problems in one way or another. And the reason that these problems persist and are so pervasive is that to admit our real feelings is, for many of us, a terrifying thing to do.

By the time we have developed some of the more serious consequences of feelings diseases, we are in such a state of denial that it is next to impossible to get us to admit that we even have a problem.

"Things will get better in my marriage when we move away from our relatives. Then I'll have time to devote to my family."

"I just need this Valium to help me through the holidays. Then I'll stop using it so often."

"I know my husband needs to go to sexual addiction treatment, but it's just not the right time to have all that turmoil in our lives. Things are going okay and he's not going out every night. We'll do it this summer when we have the time and energy."

"I know my daughter's been binging and purging (bulimia), but since she's told us about it, she hasn't done it for two weeks. I really don't think it will be a problem anymore."

What all of these people are doing is denying their feelings. In dysfunctional systems, we learn early and we learn well, that to survive in the system we must pay a "small" price—we learn to deny, ignore or escape our feelings. We learn to shut down that gnawing little voice inside of us that keeps saying, "You hurt, damn it. It's time to do something." So we go about our daily business, learning to "hope" that things will get better, while that little voice (our feelings) continues to send us messages.

When we ignore it long enough, the messages become manifest in our own bodies and in the behavior of our spouses and children. Our feelings become "acted out" in our headaches, stomachaches, ulcers, fatigue, depression and helplessness. They become "acted out" by our children in power struggles, compulsive disorders, shyness, anger and chemical abuse. And persist we must, we tell ourselves. "If I can just hold out a little longer, things will get better."

One of our favorite sayings, which we use in our therapy groups, is, "Insanity is doing the same thing and expecting different results." So while admitting our true feelings to ourselves and others is frightening for what might happen, the long term impact of not admitting them is disastrous.

We are reminded of the couple who vowed never to get "too angry" with each other because they had both come from angry, combative families. After 15 years of apparent bliss and marital harmony, their marriage ended up in our office filled with uncontrollable rage—rage composed of 15 years of normal irritations and resentments that had been denied and hidden by their well-intentioned vow. Their daughter was suicidal and their son was flunking out of school, and they hadn't the foggiest notion of what was going wrong.

All during the first session they repeatedly reminded us of their vow and how hard they had worked to keep it all these years. It was painfully apparent, we should add, that the little voices inside of them knew better, and were looking for a way to break the vow without breaking the marriage.

Inability to identify feelings and inability to express them are two of the key diagnostic features of dysfunctional families or individuals.

"I'm not angry!" he yells, gritting his teeth.

"Oh ... I'm okay ..." she says with a flat, emotionless, depressed tone of voice.

One of the most common statements in the early stages of therapy is, "Why do you keep asking me how I feel? I don't know how I feel. I just don't know." Later on, when we have begun to actually identify those feelings, we say, "Yes, I'm very unhappy in this relationship, but if I say anything about it, she'll be hurt (or go away, or get angry at me, etc)."

We have a list of perhaps 75 "feelings words" which we sometimes give to our clients to help them figure out what's really going on inside of themselves. Actually, that list could really be reduced to just a few, as is done in many dependency treatment centers. They are:

lonely	glad
hurt	mad
sad	shame
afraid	guilty

Look at that list. It's so simple, isn't it? "What's the big deal? I know when I feel those feelings! What are you talking about? I have access to all of those feelings!" If you do, then you're in great shape. Having access to our feelings is critical in not developing a dysfunctional lifestyle. But be honest with yourself.

Lonely

Do you admit to yourself that you're *lonely* when your spouse is out of town for two weeks? Or do you exhaust yourself with parties, athletics or drugs to keep from feeling that loneliness or dealing with it in healthy ways? And if you do admit that you feel lonely, what do you do with that feeling? Do you lash out and turn it into anger telling your spouse over and over how hard it was while he or she was away, and how irresponsible it was for them to go? Do you passively make them feel guilty by moping and whining and pouting?

If you are emotionally honest with yourself, you will simply let those feelings rise to the surface. You won't react out of hurt or anger or desperation because reaction in the feelings domain usually means we have lost control of ourselves in an unhealthy way. Those feelings will remain there on the surface and you will give yourself time to think about them. Is he or she gone too much? Am I being too dependent on him or her? There is a gap here in my life. How do I want to fill it? What does that gap say about me? What does it say about our relationship? Is it healthy or unhealthy?

Hurt

What do we do with our feelings of **hurt?** Do we put ourselves down?

"I shouldn't feel hurt by her. An adult wouldn't hurt; therefore, I don't hurt. My feelings of hurt must be bad. Therefore, I am bad (immature, etc.). Therefore, I won't let myself feel hurt now. I'll pretend I don't."

Or do we convert the hurt into anger? "Okay, Buster! You want to play hardball? I'll play hardball. No S.O.B. like you is going to hurt me! Take that! And that! And that!"

Or maybe our way of handling hurt is to be passively manipulative. With downturned, puppydog eyes, we mope around the house, sleep a lot, say we don't feel well, and moan incessantly to the other person about how hurtful they have been.

Either extreme is dysfunctional. Overreaction and underreaction to our feelings are opposite sides of the same coin, and they both produce the same net result—denial of our true feelings and an unsatisfying outcome from our interaction with the other person.

Sadness

Have you ever felt uncomfortable at a funeral, or felt uncomfortable with people's reactions toward you at a funeral? Unless you are at the funeral purely for a business reason, the most probable feeling that you will have is **sadness**.

Terry Kellogg calls sadness "the healing feeling." To feel sad, we must also let ourselves feel powerless. Sadness is the normal, healthy response to loss. The loss may be a parent who has died, a friend who has moved away or a house that has been burned down. Sadness feels empty at first but eventually becomes the fuel for renewed hope and existence. Sadness lets us cry without feeling ashamed. It lets us take the time to say goodbye. And best of all, it does not require that we do much of anything to be appropriate for the situation.

We feel so uncomfortable at funerals because we don't let ourselves have our sadness.

Wouldn't it feel wonderful if the next time we experienced a great loss, our friend or relative would simply walk up to us, hug us and say, "I feel sad." Not, "I feel sad for you." Just, "I feel sad." That would be all that we would need. It says that you are with me. It says that you are human. It says that we are all helpless in the face of death. It says that we're all in this together. It is affirming, honest, real and deep. Nothing else really needs to be said.

Afraid

What about **afraid**? Been afraid lately? "Not me! I'm a man! Men don't feel fear!"

In our work with couples, a large portion of the anger we hear being expressed is actually *denied fear*.

"I'm sick and tired of this women's liberation stuff," he yells. "I'm just as liberated as the next guy, but she's being irresponsible by going back to college while the kids are still in school, and quite frankly, I've had it up to here!"(Which in many relationships, translates into: "I'm afraid she'll get out into the world and meet someone else whom she finds more attractive than me.")

Being therapists, we hear a lot of this one, too. "Oh, George, what the hell are you doing still going to that stupid men's group of yours? I mean, I'm really getting sick and tired of all this therapy crap. You're gone one night a week for that and one night a week for work. When are you going to act like a man and take care of things at home like you're supposed to?" (Which translates into: "I'm afraid that you'll get healthy and see my anger for what it really is . . . fear.")

Is it scary when you have a fight with your spouse and you have to leave for work before it's resolved? Is it scary when your lover tells you that there's something wrong with the relationship? How about when you can't pay the bills this month? Do you scream at your spouse and passively ignore the children? Or do you sit down with your spouse after the children have gone to bed and simply say, "You know, Sue, I'm a little scared about our money situation, and I just need to share that with you right now." It sounds awfully corny on paper, but it sure beats scaring everyone else in the house with a load of unreal anger.

Glad

Do you feel **glad**? "Of course I do!"

About what? "Well . . . uh . . .well . . . I'm glad to be alive . . . how's that?"

That's a good start. What else? "Well . . . I don't know . . . I'm glad that . . ."

Many of us actually have trouble feeling glad. "I feel glad that I got that promotion, but I'd better not feel too glad because it might not work out."

"I feel glad that I got accepted to graduate school, but I'd better not be too glad because they didn't want me to go to graduate school."

"I feel glad that Jimmy's team won the baseball tournament, but I'd better not feel too glad because Frank never won a tournament when he was a kid and he's been competing with Jimmy ever since he was born."

Sometimes it's hard to feel glad because we never saw anyone close to us feel glad when we were growing up, leaving us with the feeling that "glad" is awfully "bad."

Garrison Keillor (radio personality and author) has got many miles from this midwestern stoicism theme.

Actually, it's not so much that glad is bad. Rather, it's that life is a very serious place to be and if we're going to get through it, we'd darned well better be serious. When those who raise us don't have access to a certain feeling, like "gladness," we learn to fit into the system by not having access to that feeling either. And looking at the big picture, it seems like such a minor oversight. I feel everything else except "glad." So what? Six out of seven ain't bad. True, except for one "big picture" oversight.

When one of our emotions gets clogged, the rest have a tendency to get clogged also, because who we are is what we feel, and when one spontaneous human feeling that we have is not allowed, we begin to question the appropriateness of our other human feelings. After awhile, we're never quite sure if what is in our emotional core is good or not. And when we start to judge the "goodness" or "badness" of our feelings (not our actions), then we're in emotional trouble.

Our feelings are simply our feelings and they will always be there flowing spontaneously from within us. What we think about them and what we do with them are another matter.

An emotionally honest person can say, "I feel glad that you have come to visit me," and when you leave, they will say, "I'm sad to see you go." An emotionally garbled person will say upon your arrival, "Why don't you visit more often? You never do anything for me! Mrs. Jones' children visit twice a month. What's the matter with you? You never did appreciate what we did for you." Hey! What happened to glad?

Mad

Mad. For many of us, this is the only emotion. For others, it's the only one we don't allow ourselves. Anger is paradoxically frightening and liberating. It can be a deceptive con, a trick to hide all other emotions. It can get us out of a jam quicker than anything else. It relieves us of responsibility. ("It's his fault that I ran into him.") It can make us feel right whether we're right or wrong. But if your anger is covering up another emotion, do yourself a big favor. Turn it off absolutely and completely for awhile and take the ultimate risk—see if there's another emotion underneath it that's just dying to get out.

To know if this is true, you will have to spend some time alone with yourself without books or television or friends or spouses/lovers or children.

You will have to let yourself be alone, if only for a few minutes, in which you are so alone that your deepest connection to life itself is the awareness of your own heartbeat inside of your chest. If there are other emotions there, let yourself feel them. If after that you still feel angry, then go ahead and let yourself feel it. In other words, if anger is your game, try playing by a different set of rules. If it isn't, you'd better shoot for playing with a full deck.

In addictions circles there are those of us who can get angry and who feel comfortable with it, and there are those of us who can't. If you're "good" at anger, take the plunge and try something new, like hurt or sadness or fear. If you aren't good at "anger," why not give it a shot? In other words, there are a lot of us human beings who have learned so well to be "good" that we don't know how to be ourselves.

You "typical addicts" out there don't want us to steal your thunder. We don't stand up for ourselves and then we lean on you to stand up for us, because you're so good at "doing anger." So we wind up conning ourselves and conning you.

The game becomes, "Do my dirty work for me, and I'll do your dirty work for you!" But it also becomes, "I'll be powerless for myself, let you express my anger for me, and then resent you for taking my power away from me."

Why not try this? "I think I need to get angry about this myself. It doesn't mean I don't love you or need you. I just need to claim my own power. In fact, I'll have more power to love you when I'm done." Can you buy that?

Shame

Shame. It is felt by many therapists nowadays that shame is at the very base of all addictions. Gershen Kaufman (1980), a psychologist who did some pioneering writing about shame, believes that shame comes from damaging the interpersonal bridge between two people, especially when one of those people is more powerful than the other. Shame comes from not being able to depend on someone. It is a feeling of being exposed as helpless. It can best be expressed as feeling worth less (than I did before that bridge was broken). That is, we feel worthless. "*I made a mistake*" becomes "*I am a mistake.*"

Imagine a child who is criticized by her parent. The criticism breaks the bridge between parent and child. The relationship suddenly comes into question.

"I have done something awful," we say to ourselves, "and Mommy doesn't love me (approve of me, care for me, etc.) anymore. She won't be there for me now when I need her."

We feel ashamed of ourselves. We feel worthless, We feel helpless. We feel scared.

To help clarify the dynamic of *shame induction,* imagine yourself surrounded by all of your loved ones. You are in the center and they are encircling you. Each and every one of them is pointing a finger at you, eyes glaring, saying, "Shame, shame, shame on you! You are bad! You are stupid! You are ugly! You are clumsy!"

That is the essence of shame. It is ostracism. It is being cut off from the group. From the human race. From your most precious support. A child can be corrected without being shamed. But when the inner core of the child is left with a haunting voice inside saying, "I am bad," then we are speaking of shame.

As adults this core of shame is usually well hidden from us (not necessarily from others). We hide it with anger or sadness or depression or, for many of us, with one or more addictions.

"She didn't return my phone call? Who needs her? I'll go out with the guys and get drunk."

"The boss didn't like my report? I'll fix him! Don't get mad, get even!"

"Mom and Dad don't like the way I dress? They don't like the shape of my chin? Who needs them? I'll just sleep around with all the boys. They're interested in me."

"My husband doesn't think that I'm spontaneous enough? Who needs to be spontaneous? I can work circles around him and make three times what he makes. Work addiction? You must be kidding. I'm just not a loser!"

A friend of ours, John Holtzermann, describes shame thus: "I passed by the mirror and was surprised to see that it thought enough of me to reflect my image."

Shame also comes from being spoiled because we never learn to be self-reliant and autonomous. We remain overly dependent on our families for a sense of well-being, which leaves us helpless and paralyzed as we face the outside world. Parents who give their children too much, who do too much for them and who protect their children from life's pain are not doing their children a favor. *Spoiling a child is a form of emotional abuse.*

Guilt

Guilt is a tricky one for a lot of us because there is healthy guilt and there is unhealthy guilt, and often it is hard to know the difference.

Healthy guilt lets us know when we have authentically done something to hurt someone else, and it provides the energy and drive for us to want to correct the hurt.

Unhealthy, inauthentic guilt tells us that we have done something wrong when we really haven't, and thus it provides a lot of energy and drive to keep us paralyzed.

Anytime we step outside of ourselves and make something happen, we are open to feeling guilty. But is it appropriate to feel guilty because we want to go back to school and get a college diploma, just because our husband wants us home every night to give him backrubs? Should we feel guilty for not wanting to be around our parents when they physically and emotionally abuse us? We don't think so.

Feelings awareness is a key to recovery from dysfunctional family systems. We invite you to have your feelings because they are truly the Little Child Within who needs to be nurtured, loved, listened to, affirmed, held and protected. Have reverence for your feelings, and you will begin to have reverence for yourself.

12

The Secrets

It is said that every family has its skeletons in the closet. In the public domain politicians are perhaps the most sensitive to this fact. Many a career has been slowed, diverted or stopped because of the public disclosure of some past impropriety that everyone including the politican thought had long since been forgotten. In the domain of family and intimate relationships, it is our closely kept secrets that can kill us.

Secrets can be about our feelings, our thoughts or our behavior. They have a great deal of shame attached to them, or we wouldn't be expending so much energy keeping them secret. Finding a safe place to disclose those secrets is the key to overcoming addiction and family dysfunction.

Ask any recovering alcoholic family what it was like "in the old days" when everyone spent all of their time figuring out how to hide Dad's alcoholism. Children make excuses to their friends about why they can't have anyone over to the house. Mom tells the children that "Dad's tired." Dad's parents become adept at the use of "creative euphemisms," such as "He just went into the kitchen to have a little nip."

The perplexing thing about these secrets is that they are only secret at one level of consciousness. At other levels, everyone knows the secret and everyone in the family becomes part of the game.

Or take the family where healthy anger is frowned upon. Everyone walks around with smiles plastered on their faces all the time. I step on your toe, you smile. I need some time alone but you don't want me to, and I smile. You forget to pick up Suzy from school, and I smile.

In a family where no one is allowed to use anger in a healthy way to set boundaries, the secret is our feelings. At a very superficial level of consciousness, we are all very happy and smiley. Underneath it, we are all angry as the dickens. The end result is craziness.

Our non-verbal language is saying "I'm mad. I'm very mad." Everyone else picks up this non-verbal language, but they pick it up unconsciously and non-verbally. Thus, everyone is walking around living in two worlds simultaneously and feeling crazy. As the secret becomes more and more embedded in the fabric of the family, individual family members begin to "act out the secret."

Suzy does poorly in school and gets depressed a lot. Dad worries about Suzy a lot. Mom spends all of her time frantically trying to cheer everyone up. Jimmy gets into drugs or masturbates a lot. If they get into therapy (ostensibly to help the family member who is identified as the one with "the real problem"), the therapist will probably ask if anyone ever gets angry. A resounding chorus from all family members will be, "No. We don't believe in getting angry at each other. We love each other."

Secrets are kept outside of the family, too. Even trained professionals help us keep our unhealthy secrets. Not a week seems to go by that we don't get someone who is clearly alcoholic or obese, and who has been in therapy before, but who was *never* asked about their eating or drinking behavior.

We know of a man who had spent $15,000 on therapy with three different therapists, and not one of them had ever asked him about the fact that he weighed 325 pounds. It wasn't surprising to find out that in fact this man had learned to control his secret so well from such an early age that he couldn't remember anyone ever talking to him about his weight in all of his 42 years of living.

We asked, "Have you ever tried to do anything about your obesity?" and he said, "No, I've been too ashamed of my weight my entire life to ever ask for help."

Months later, and well into his recovery from compulsive overeating, he shared with us how that one simple question represented the beginning of a new life for him. It had exposed the secret and removed its burden from his life.

Covert Behavior

Psychotherapists speak of needing to make the covert overt. Overt behavior is that which can be seen. Covert behavior, thoughts or feelings are those which cannot be seen directly.

We explain to our clients that in unhealthy families, the most important action is really going on underneath the table. Above the table we are all lightness and smiles. Beneath the table we are angry, frightened, ashamed, lonely, confused and so on. Above the table we are in control, composed, relaxed. Beneath the table we are feeling out of control, tense or terrified. Because of the shame attached to our secrets, the fear of being emotionally naked in front of our loved ones is what keeps the covert hidden.

"If we don't talk about Dad's depression, maybe it will go away."

"If we don't talk about Mom's alcoholism, maybe it will go away."

"If we don't talk about work addiction, maybe he'll eventually spend more time at home."

When we get down to the real root of the problem, what we really don't want to talk about is how we feel about it. Some families are great when it comes to talking about someone else's problem. "My husband doesn't like sex. That's our problem." But how do you feel about it? What does it mean to you? Do you ever fear that he doesn't like you?

Very often covert issues will come out in a relationship around issues of money and sex. Couples will battle for years about how their money is spent, when the real covert issue which needs to come to the surface and become overt is that they aren't getting their emotional needs met in the relationship. But that's so scary to say. If I say that, she might run away. She might be so hurt that she'll die. Or she might be so incensed that she'll leave me. Or she might think that I'm petty and stupid for feeling that way. If I expose my true feelings, I'll be shamed by her.

Sex is a powerful arena for acting out our covert issues in destructive ways. I am angry at you, so I don't want to make love. Or I am angry at you and want to control and possess you, so all I want to do is have sex. I am so dependent and unsure of myself that I need to make love with you all the time, and if we don't, it confirms my sense of worthlessness.

The power of secrets in the maintenance of our symptoms cannot be over stressed. When someone is work-addicted, there's a secret beneath it. When someone is addicted to television or exercise, there is an emotional secret lurking beneath the surface.

Removing the addictive agent is only the beginning of recovery from addiction. Getting to the secret and letting it come out without shame or blame is the key to healthy recovery. If this is true, why don't families just realize this and get it out in the open? We are asked this over and over by people with grade school educations all the way up to Ph.D.'s.

Her husband was beating her up all those years, and we never knew it. And he's a doctor! How could that happen? Why didn't she say something? Well, think about it. If you lived in a $350,000 house, drove a Jaguar and dressed like Jackie Onassis, would you want everyone in the community to know that your husband was beating you up?

"Oh, and by the way, after you're finished tuning up the Jaguar, would you sit down and talk with me about the beatings I've been getting for the past 10 years?"

Many psychologists believe that all of our behavior serves a purpose, and we tend to agree. The secrets that we have learned to keep may have served a useful purpose once. At age seven, on a long car trip you wet your pants because you couldn't wait for the next gas station. Everyone feels badly for you, you get cleaned up and then the trip proceeds happily. Nobody wants to focus on it or make a big deal of it because they know how embarrassed you felt. The family is tactful and respectful and that's the end of it. And it never happens again.

Or Dad goes on a camping trip and drinks too much and makes a fool of himself. It never happened before and it's not likely to happen again. He feels sheepish about it, shares it with the family when he gets back, they all have a little laugh about it and then they go on. No problem.

Unhealthy secrets begin in much the same way. Mom and Dad have a rip-roaring fight until 1:00 in the morning, and you go to school the next day worried and tense. You don't want anyone at school thinking that something is wrong with your family (and therefore, by implication, something wrong with you), so you don't say anything about it. You come home from school that evening to find that Mom and Dad have worked out their problem, and that's that. No big deal.

But it turns out that they haven't worked out the problem. Five days later they have another late-night fight. And then two days after that. Then Dad leaves for a few days.

Your stomach is in knots. You can't concentrate. Your grades start to suffer. You're sad a lot. You wish things would get better. You wish there was someone to talk to about it. But you can't. Your shame kicks in and you feel too embarrassed to say anything. Maybe Mom and Dad told you not to say anything to anyone. Or maybe you just start to hope and pray that if you ignore it long enough, it will just go away. Over the days, weeks and months, the secret becomes an unhealthy secret cemented into your unconscious, seemingly forever.

Or maybe Dad is extremely rigid and dogmatic when it comes to television. He grudgingly lets you watch television, but he covertly lets you know that he's not pleased with you for watching it. You don't even watch it very much. After awhile, you watch it but you talk as if you really hate it. But you keep watching.

As an adult, you can't stop watching TV. You don't have any true friendships. You're lost without television. But when the topic comes up, you're quick to say that you don't watch much TV.

One secret is that you watch TV. But an even deeper one is that Dad has shamed you, and you hate him for it. That carefully protected secret will come out years later with your own son. You'll criticize him constantly for something. Maybe it will be his hair or his clothes or his interest in music or sports or his table manners or the amount of television he watches. You won't know why you're doing it. You won't even see that it's damaging him. You'll simply feel that something is terribly, deeply wrong with him.

And what is really going on, underneath the table, is that you still feel that there is something terribly deeply wrong with you. The secret is about your own shame, which was the shame that was passed down to you by your father.

Secrets in families can be overwhelmingly difficult to get out into the open. In cases of incest or sexual abuse, it may take years or even several generations before the secret is revealed. And in many cases the secret simply doesn't get out in time.

At least once a year we read in our local newspaper about the successful doctor or lawyer or star high school student who went home one day and blew his brains out with a gun, sometimes taking the rest of his family with him. In each case there was a very important secret that was embedded within the family. Secret taboos against "failure," against being masculine or feminine, or secret taboos limiting the range of feelings that we can allow ourselves.

Over the years we become so divided within ourselves that we don't know how we really feel anymore. We become like two people: our outside mask and our inner self. Being split in two emotionally, we may eventually become split in two physically (in a metaphorical sense) and die.

One of the reasons that 12-Step programs (such as Alcoholics Anonymous) are so successful in helping us with our addictions is that they begin to allow us to come to grips with our secrets and our shame. Ask anyone how they felt going to their first A.A. meeting or going to treatment for cocaine addiction. They felt that it was the longest walk of their life. As if they were approaching death row. It is an admission of powerlessness (which we confuse with helplessness and failure until we begin to recover). It feels so shaming.

"I am so embarrassed about having to do this," we say. Our spouses say, "But I just don't think I can tolerate the humiliation of being married to an addict."

And yet usually within days of taking that first step, most people who work their programs courageously begin to feel a tremendous surge of relief. The weight of carrying all of that shame and fear of humiliation is no longer so heavy. We have exposed ourselves, surrounded by people, encircled by them, and we have bared our deepest, most frightening secret, and no one shamed us. No one pointed their fingers at us and said, "Shame, shame, shame on you!" No one said "We are stupid or ugly or clumsy or worthless or bad" because we admitted we were alcoholic or co-dependent or sex addicted.

Certainly, there will be plenty of people "out there" who will perhaps be quick to judge us and criticize us. But with the strength of a healthy surrogate family system behind us in the form of a 12-step or therapy group, we are able to let go of our secrets and our shame and, therefore, our dysfunction.

The most common secrets we see are about:
1. Addictions
2. Incest or Sexual Abuse
3. Physical Abuse
4. Suicide
5. Perceived Failure
6. Mental Illness

13

What Happens to
Our Identity?

We have thus far described what we believe to be the family system's roots of our dysfunctional lifestyles. But what happens to us in terms of being a whole person? What does family dysfunction do to our sense of self, to our inner clarity, to our sense of who we are? These are all questions of identity.

By *identity* we mean one's self-definition. We mean self-knowledge of, and commitment to, a set of values, beliefs, behaviors and lifestyle. Our identities include what we like and don't like, what risks we are willing to take, what we believe in, both religiously and philosophically, as well as politically and scientifically. Identity includes our sexual behaviors and feelings, our career choices, and satisfaction or dissatisfaction with them, whether we choose to be parents or not. Whether we choose to go to church or not. Whether we choose to be in a spouse or lover-type of relationship. What we like to do with our free time. Whether we are alcoholic or cocaine addicted or sexually addicted or running addicts are also part of our identities, as is whether or not we are recovering from these addictions or are still acting them out. The famous developmental theorist Erik Erikson (Erikson 1963,

1968) devoted a great deal of his life to the study of identity formation. He generated a series of eight psychosocial stages to help us pull together and explain how human personalities grow and change from birth to death. These stages, and the work that Erikson has done around the identity stage, offer us a powerful mechanism for looking at what happens to us if we grow up in a dysfunctional family system.

Even in a very healthy family, the task of growing up and leaving home with a clear identity of our own is a difficult task. Somewhere between the ages of 18 and 25 or so, our main developmental task is to come to terms with who we are as a separate adult. This task hinges on the relatively successful fulfillment of four earlier developmental challenges, according to Erikson, and actually includes issues and skills from earlier tasks.

The four stages leading up to the *identity crisis are*:

0–1½	Trust versus Mistrust
1½–3	Autonomy versus Shame, Doubt
3–6	Initiative versus Guilt
6–18	Industry versus Inferiority

These stages represent *psychosocial crises* or tasks, and each one builds upon one another. This means that if the stones at the base of the foundation are weak, or almost nonexistent, the entire structure will be weak or actually collapse later on. In the same way, if we have developmental stages that were handled less than ideally early on in life, then we will run into a lot of trouble later as we try to grow up and become an adult.

These crises or stages are broadly defined. They are labeled according to when they *first* became a major task in our lives. As you peruse the list of stages, you will see that they are tasks and challenges that face all of us throughout our lives, *not* just when they *first* appear. And lastly, each stage and the skills that we learned as we pass through it become incorporated into the later stages.

For example, the *Initiative versus Guilt* stage includes issues of Trust and Autonomy. These Trust and Autonomy issues are age-appropriate, though, so it does not mean that to take the initiative we have to go back to infancy and breast-feed again, or that we have to learn how to walk again.

1. Trust versus Mistrust

The first challenge facing us as human beings is to develop a basic sense of trust in the world. This means that we are left with a feeling that we can rely on those we need, that the world is basically a safe place to be and that we can survive. If our basic needs for food and shelter and affection and touch are met during early infancy, then we most likely will develop a sense of trust. But trust means more than just that. It also means that we can trust that things will work out in the end, even if we don't get what we need right away.

A two-year-old, for example, does not have to be the tyrant of the house, demanding and getting everything they want on the spot. If our two-year-old is told that they will have to wait a few minutes until dinner is ready, or that they cannot have everything that they see in a store, it will not erode their basic sense of trust.

In fact, if we go overboard on giving things to our kids, we actually undermine their sense of trust, because we are setting them up to live in a world that doesn't exist. Few people in this world, if any, get everything they want when they want it. And thus, one of the most important themes of development throughout our entire lives begins right here, in the first stage. And that theme is: *Too much or too little of what we need is no good.*

Things that leave a child with a basic sense of mistrust about the world and themselves include overt physical or emotional abuse, neglect or abandonment. These are extremes. The more subtle forces that operate during this stage are inconsistent care (babysitting or daycare do not have to be inconsistent), tension and stress in parents that is communicated by inability to be nurturing, spontaneous or comfortable with our infants. Too much overt conflict can upset young children, also overprotective parents who do not allow their young children to explore their world and their own bodies in normal ways. Infants need to learn that they can depend on us, that the world will not always give them what they want and that they can still be "okay" about it. They do not need to be scared, spoiled, neglected or abused. A basic sense of mistrust leaves us with severe *fear of abandonment* issues.

2. Autonomy versus Shame, Doubt

The issue to be resolved here is one of separateness. Between one-and-a-half and three years of age, our children become mobile, they learn the power of language for defining their separateness (the word "no!" for example), and their task is to begin to become autonomous while still feeling safe and trusting of the world.

Our two-year-olds toddle off to explore things by themselves. They exert their will. They get into power struggles with us. And because they are still so vulnerable and dependent upon us, they need to be able to do this and still know that they can run back to us for comfort if their independence leads them into things that are scary or hurtful.

Imagine your two-year-old running into the house in tears, crying that "a big dog walked through the yard and growled at me!" The dog represents a threat to our sense of autonomy: "I can't go out into the world by myself because it's too dangerous," we feel. If a parent simply affirms us and our feelings by saying, "Boy, I'll bet that was scary," and makes us feel safe again by giving us a hug and letting us have our feelings without being judgmental, then soon we will be ready to go back into the world again.

If, on the other hand, our parents *shame* us ("Big boys don't cry," "I told you not to go outside by yourself"), or simply aren't available enough to us during these times (by not being there enough or by ignoring us), then we will begin to internalize shame and doubt.

Likewise, we can experience shame and doubt if we are too restricted in our attempts to be separate individuals. Parents who mean well but who are overprotective of us, never give us the chance to separate from them. Also, if our parents are too permissive, giving us few guidelines on how to behave in the world outside of our homes, we can wind up feeling shame and doubt. Parents who let their children climb on the furniture, break things a lot, and generally tyrannize the household produce children who get shamed a lot when they go to other people's homes or when they go to school.

Again, the rule of thumb here is one of balance. We need to set limits and boundaries on our children at this age, but we also need to allow enough freedom and safety for our children for them to want to begin separating from us.

3. Initiative versus Guilt

This stage has a lot to do with our ability to start things, make things happen and stretch beyond our current capabilities. Those of us who are "stuck," who can't get out of a rut, who can't make decisions, have issues with this stage.

Between three and six years of age, we begin to want to be more like adults. We want to go into the kitchen and cook something the way Mom and Dad do. Or we want to go into the garage and get the saw and build something. We want to initiate things. This has much to do with self-expansion, of going beyond. If you think about it, anytime we try to initiate something on our own, there is always the possibility of someone else feeling put out, let down, disappointed or "hurt." When they let us know about it, we feel guilty.

Dad gets a bee in his bonnet and decides to tear out the wall in the kitchen and do some remodeling while Mom is on a business trip. Mom comes home, doesn't like it and says, "How could you begin such a major change in my kitchen without first consulting me?" Dad feels some shame, but he will also feel guilt. He has "done something wrong," violated a moral principle of some kind.

The task at ages three to six is to begin internalizing principles of right and wrong, but not to the detriment of our ability to initiate things.

If my children try to rebuild the engine of my car at this age, I need to convey to them that this is inappropriate behavior because they aren't old enough to do it properly, and besides, it's "my" car, not "theirs." It's how I convey that message that is so important.

If I say, "You really let down Dad. I am surprised that you would do this. You really hurt me by doing it," my children will indeed not do it again.

But if I use this method of discipline on a regular basis, I will produce very well-behaved children who won't be able to get themselves out of a wet paper bag when they are adults. They will be "nice," but that's about it. They will be filled with guilt and indecision. They will always focus on who will be affected by their actions without ever considering their own needs or feelings. They will become over-focused on not violating all of these rules they internalize. Big rules, middle-sized rules and pointless tiny rules.

4. Industry versus Inferiority

This stage involves developing a sense of competence and confidence around those skills necessary for survival in our culture. These skills include the three R's, but go well beyond them.

Certainly, we need academic skills to get by in this world, but all too often the range of skills that are reinforced in our schools and at home is painfully narrow. Not every child will be a whiz at math, English or physics. Not every child will become another Picasso or Beethoven. Some children will become excellent mechanics, if allowed to be. Others will become well-adjusted accountants. Others, plumbers. These school-age years are critical for a child's sense of worth. They are also critical for a child's ability to identify with, and bond with, older people who know how to do things. So it is a compliment to us, and to our child, if he forms an attachment to a friend's Dad, who is showing him how to work on cars. It is okay if our daughter likes her English teacher, and gets excited about what the teacher is teaching her.

It is *not* okay if our children have no room to feel good about themselves during these years. It is *not* okay to compare one child to another one in the family. It is *not* okay to feel jealous or possessive of our children just because they like a friend's Mom or Dad. If we feel jealous, we need psychotherapy to work through the dysfunction that we are experiencing.

It is okay if one child excels at math, another excels at drawing, and another excels at auto mechanics. It is okay if our children feel good about themselves, even though they haven't got straight A's or a B-average or whatever our criteria for success happen to be. We know many wealthy successful people who never finished high school or college. We know many happy successful "non-wealthy" people, too. Some of them have high school diplomas, some have college diplomas and some have Ph.D.'s.

The basic skills that are learned during this stage are how to work, how to get along with other people, how to be social and political people, how to get what we need out of life without alienating everyone around us, and how to feel good about what we do. The specifics of how we do that are not nearly as important as doing it somehow. In rigid dysfunctional families, there is only one right way to do it. In healthy families, there are literally hundreds of ways to do it.

Identity versus Identity Confusion

As we said earlier, the above four stages bring us to the first adult stage of our development, which is called *Identity versus Identity Confusion* (also called Identity Diffusion) somewhere between the ages of 18 and 29, depending upon how much formal education we get, economic factors and family system factors. Erikson and researchers, who have studied his theories, believe that there are two key parts to achieving a clear identity: *crisis* and *commitment*.

Erikson felt that it was not possible to be a healthy adult with a clear sense of self without going through a *psychosocial moratorium*, which is just a fancy way to say a period of questioning and rebellion.

We must question our religious beliefs, the values with which we were raised, career choices that our parents may have overtly or covertly made for us, lifestyle preferences, and the like. We may come back to those childhood beliefs after this period of questioning, but we won't be children when we do and we won't be doing it "just because someone told us it was the right way to live or think." Or we may not come back to our childhood beliefs, choosing other ways to think and act than the ones that were given to us by our parents.

One fact remains: if we don't go through this *crisis* period of rebellion and questioning, we won't get through the Identity Stage. It is this fact that causes dysfunctional families so many problems when their children near adulthood.

The *commitment* part of identity means that we must make clear choices about our beliefs and lifestyles eventually, and that our choices must be more than just verbal ones. We must act on them.

A person who chooses monogamy but has extramarital affairs all the time is not committed to monogamy as a lifestyle. A person who claims to be a Christian but who treats his family and employees like dirt is not living his beliefs—he is only talking about them. This kind of empty rhetoric is a double message and a double bind for the members of the family, and it will eventually backfire.

Children whose parents say one thing but do another eventually lose all respect for their parents.

Based on the depth of the crisis we have had, and the strength of our commitment, Erikson has delineated four possible identity types or outcomes during this stage. (For an extended discussion of these types, and how they are related to co-dependency, see Friel, Subby and Friel, 1985.) These four types are:

1. Identity Achieved

We have been through an identity crisis with regard to work, religion, sexuality, political beliefs and lifestyle. We have also made clear commitments to our current choices, so that our feelings, beliefs and actions are congruent. That is, they match. Do we have to have a clear commitment to all parts of ourselves and our choices? No, but the fewer we have, the less likely it is that we are identity achieved.

2. Moratorium

We are in the crisis period. We are actively searching. We are trying on different hats. We are dating different people. We are trying out different careers or college majors. But there is something systematic and directed to our search. We have not made clear commitments yet.

3. Foreclosed

Our hunch is that probably close to 50% of us are in this state. If we are Adult Children who have not broken through our denial yet, then we are most likely in this state or in the last one, below. Foreclosure means that we seem to have a clear set of commitments, but we never really went through a crisis period to get there.

We go into adulthood wearing the same childhood hats that we've always had on but the hat is on an adult body. We wear adult suits and ties and dresses and we say adult words, do adult things and tell ourselves that we believe adult beliefs—but we are not truly adults because we have not yet grown up.

Why? Because growing up is scary. It hurts. It is sometimes lonely. It means saying goodbye to childhood and making peace with whatever childhood fantasies, as well as demons, we may have grown up with. We Adult Children have so many demons that getting out of foreclosure is very hard to do. Actually, denial and fear are what keep us stuck.

"My husband is not like my dad," we assert. "Dad was a drunk. My husband is a hardworking, responsible man!" (Adult Child Translation: "My husband is an unavailable workaholic, but because he's not a drunk, it must be better.") That's how our denial works.

Later in the marriage we may say, "My husband's not available to me emotionally, but what else can I do? He's a good provider. I have all the things a woman could ever want. And besides, I don't know how I would ever provide for myself." That's how the fear works against us.

Getting out of foreclosure is like standing on the edge of a cliff on a pitch-black, moonless night, and then jumping off without knowing whether the cliff is three feet high or 100 feet high. It is not something we should be doing without a strong support system in place beforehand.

Making this kind of change is also risky because what usually happens is that we get a lot of flack from those around us. Translation: We get guilted and shamed. "She's crazy. That's all there is to it. Any woman would just die to be married to him!" (And she is dying, emotionally.)

"How could you dare to go back to college. What about me and the kids? Who will be there to do the cooking and the laundry? Who will be there to make love with me every night?" Translation: Dad may be sexually addicted, or at the very least, female-dependent and the children have been spoiled to the point of not knowing how to run the washer and dryer or cook a meal.

Leaving foreclosure behind brings censure from others simply because it is a time of turmoil, too. We even see professional therapists labeling clients as "dysfunctional" or "neurotic" when in fact, they are simply entering a healthy moratorium stage in their lives. Translation: They are taking the big risk of becoming adults. More power to them!

4. Identity Confused (Diffused)

When we are in this state, we are in constant crisis but it is different from when we are in a moratorium. The crisis goes in circles. There is no direction to it. We jump from one lover to the next, from one job or career to the next, from one set of beliefs to the next and from one lifestyle to the next. We are lost souls, wandering the earth looking for a sense of security in a way that we never got it. Some of us here are offenders and addicts who hurt a lot of people in the process of wandering.

In college we may have been the Party King or Queen, but we never quite get out of that role. Or we are the rigid, religious fundamentalist whose entire identity is defined and controlled by something outside of ourselves. While some of us here may speak of being easygoing free spirits, we are far from that. We cannot tolerate differences of opinion because any other opinion would threaten our very sense of self and that is not tolerable. When we are identity achieved, a good chunk of our sense of self is comfortably inside of us, and cannot be threatened by someone else's point of view.

People ask us how so many people could follow Jim Jones to Guyana and then commit mass suicide with him at his command. We believe that they were identity confused, and that they needed Jim Jones so much for their own self-definition that they were willing to give up the very essence of their self-definition—their own lives.

Getting beyond foreclosure or confusion requires that we have strong, healthy building blocks when we reach adolescence. It also requires that we look at our childhoods, have our feelings about our childhoods, re-evaluate both the "good" and the "bad", and take our parents off the pedestals that we had them on as children. Our parents are neither saints nor ogres—they are human beings.

To take our parents off those pedestals and "let" them be human is tremendously painful if we are Adult Children because we are strongly en-meshed with them. We are enmeshed if they were over-indulgent with us, and we are enmeshed if they were abusive and neglectful. In the latter case, we are enmeshed because we keep going back to an empty well for water but there is none there. We keep hoping and praying that it will be there, but it never is. What we are going back for is something that perhaps our parents will never be able to give us because their childhoods were abusive and neg-lectful.

As Alice Miller so aptly stated (Miller, 1987), the pain of admitting that our parents were not capable of loving us (in perfect healthy ways) is much greater than the pain of believing that we were "bad" and didn't deserve love. And so we remain foreclosed, until the pain becomes so great that we must change.

In other words, our symptoms, our addictions and our pain are really our allies. They tell us when the Little Child Within has had enough and wants some help to grow up.

14

Intimacy
and Beyond

Erikson's next stage is called Intimacy versus Isolation, and it is in the arena of intimacy that so many of us Adult Children experience our most painful crises.

We like to define intimacy as the *ability to be in relationship with someone without sacrificing our identity in the process.* It is the last part of this definition which is so crucial. While there are many types of intimacy, such as physical, sexual, intellectual, social, spiritual and the sharing of play and hobbies, intimacy in any of these domains with *loss of self on a regular basis is not intimacy—it is dependency.*

Loss of self during sex is normal and okay, but always deferring to another's wishes and never asking for what we like is not okay and it is not healthy. If we really don't care what movie we go to, then letting someone else choose the movie makes sense. If we do care deep down inside and still rarely state our preference, then we are being overly dependent.

The best way to truly evaluate the health of our relationships is to identify how we truly feel, which requires that we are in enough of our own recovery to let those feelings come to the surface. We have listed below how intimacy feels compared to dependent relationships.

Intimacy (Interdependent)	Dysfunctional Relationships (Dependent/Isolated)
whole	desperate
joyful	fearful
competent	anxious
interested	rejected
strong	angry
clear	confused
comfortable	abandoned
peaceful	exhausted
fulfilled	invisible
grateful	controlled
happy	used
excited	manipulated
trusting	empty
alone-ness	loneliness
together-ness	identity-less

Believe it or not, we know of several marriages and long-term friendships that can best be described by the list on the left.

Below we have outlined some of the issues and problems that seem to crop up the most in relationships between Adult Children.

Objectification

With our cups running on "empty," we have a strong tendency to make our friends and lovers into "things" that are designed to make up for our deficiencies. We objectify each other by trying to make our friends into our therapists, moms and dads or saviors.

We make each other into sex objects who are designed to make us feel momentarily better and intimate, but we lack the ability to be intimate in the much broader terms necessary for a healthy relationship. As therapists and human beings, the authors sincerely believe that true intimacy is made up of the little day-to-day actions that many of us view as "boring" until we get into recovery.

The Owe-Pay Syndrome

Another form of objectification is to do a lot of things for others to the point of burnout in the hope that they will then be indebted to us and be nice to us in return. We then proclaim loudly or softly that the other person "owes" us. We say, "Look at all I've done for you!" That statement is a red flag indicating that we are in an addictive relationship, and that we have compromised our identities and our dignity.

Communicating Feelings

As the famous psychotherapist Carl Rogers (1973) has suggested, any persistent feeling needs to be expressed, no matter how trivial it may seem at the time. In relationships that work well, these feelings are aired and dealt with before they become deep resentments. They are also shared tactfully, with respect for the other's dignity.

For example: "Tom, I need to talk to you about the amount of time we spend together. I love you very much, yet lately I have been feeling that I don't have enough time to myself, and I don't want those feelings to interfere with what I feel for you ..."

Partner Choice

Family systems theorists speak of how we re-enact our family of origins in our adult lives, so there is some truth to the old Freudian idea that we marry our father or our mother. But people get confused by this idea because they only look at the surface characteristics of themselves and Mom and Dad.

If Mom was overly emotional and clingy, we might marry someone who on the surface is strong and independent. If the systems from which we came are dysfunctional, then that strong independent woman will be foreclosed with a dependent child living within her body. When her dependency comes out, it may take the form of her being demanding, pushy, and critical. Her fear causes that, and it is no fun to be around.

Or she may reveal her dependency in letting you walk all over her—you being the offender and she being the victim. She will be competent and independent at work, and helpless in her relationship with you.

What actually happened here is that you reacted to Mom's helplessness and dependency, became the offender like your dad, and married someone who you thought was the opposite of Mom but who really wasn't. Reacting to our families of origin means that we are not free of them. They still control us if we have to react to them instead of making our own choices based on a clear identity.

Unclear Boundaries

We get tangled up in each other's lives too much. Your sadness becomes my sadness. Or I expect you to meet all of my needs and demand this. I want you to fill my cup, and I don't know how to stop asking and demanding. I push you for sex when you don't want it. I make you stay up half the night to "talk about problems." I get jealous if you have friends, especially of the opposite sex. In other words, I don't let you be you. I blame you for my unhappiness instead of doing what I need to do to become happier. We started out as separate people before we met.

If we are unrecovering Adult Children, we quickly get so tangled up that we can't have intimacy because we've lost our identity.

Separation Problems

Separation is part of life. A big part of it. Life is a continual coming together and separating. We have trouble with this because we get frightened that if the other goes away, they'll never come back. So we create lots of conflict around our separations. We fight when one of us is about to leave for a four-day business trip. Then we harangue the other upon their return. After being apart for the day, we meet at night and argue about the intimacy that we don't have.

The German poet Rilke described love as "two solitudes (that) protect and touch and greet each other." A big part of why we can't be this way is due to the next issue below, which is . . .

All The Eggs In One Basket

We invest way too much in our few close relationships. We expect our spouse or partner to be all things to us—Mother, Father, Lover, Friend, Tennis Partner, Parent of Our Children, Only Confidant, Therapist, Bridge Partner, Babysitter, Provider and . . . Nobody can be all things to one person. In one of our favorite books on the subject, *The Road Less Traveled*, Scott Peck says that we don't truly love each other unless we can live without each other (Peck, 1978), and we agree.

Control Issues

This is related to our fear of abandonment and, ultimately, to our fear of death. We are mortal. We cannot prevent our physical death, and we cannot make someone love us. The power struggles that we get into with each other are about this need to control the uncontrollable. In fact, that's what addictions are about. It is very common for us to act out our addictions much more when we are alone, or when that spouse or lover of ours is on a four-day business trip. When they are home with us, we try to control the situation by controlling them, which only pushes them farther away from us.

Handling Conflicts

Conflict in relationships is unavoidable. Whenever two people get close to each other for a while, their very separateness will lead to differences of opinion, needs or values. This is natural. In healthy relationships, these conflicts get settled. In unhealthy ones, they drag on and on and on; or both people compromise so much that they both feel bored.

Common Interests?

This one is very hard to pin down. Do we *need* to have all of the same interests? Some of the same interests? A few? Is it better to have none at all? It certainly helps to have some interests in common, just as it helps to have some of the same personality traits in common. But by no means do we have to be the same. We know of successful couples who are very similar in interests and personality, and we know of some who are very different. What seems to be most important is that we meet each other's needs in ways that are meaningful to our partner or friend, that we share a "global life view," and that the relationship is life-enhancing rather than draining for us.

Dialogue on Intimacy

We sometimes walk a fine line between love and dependency. True intimacy is a precious gift that is freely given with no strings attached. At the same time, we must have reciprocity in our relationships, which sounds at first like a contradiction. Misinterpreted, this reciprocity turns into the "Owe-Pay Syndrome" that we discussed above. Actually, it isn't.

The tough part is that we must *want* give-and-take in our relationships. There must be enough for us in the relationship to want to give something back. We cannot give something back simply because the other person demands it. And we cannot demand from another what we want from them. We can only ask. This is truly a paradox. For us Adult Children, it is the toughest paradox of all for us to transcend.

Think about the following exchange between partners:

B: I've been reading this book about intimacy between Adult Children, and it says that we have a tendency to either get enmeshed with each other or get too detached from each other. What do you think we do?

R: Hmmm . . . I don't know, I think we have a pretty good balance between the two.

B: Yeah, I guess so . . .

R: What's the matter? You sound a little sad.

B: Oh, I don't know. I mean, don't you think we get too far apart a little too often?

R: Not really. I think we have a good balance between our own separate lives and the life that we share. But obviously you don't. What's the matter?

B: I just don't think that we have that great of a relationship. Yeah, that's what I think.

R: Well, you don't have to have a fit about it! Can't we just talk it out?

B: Have a fit about it? You're being judgmental again!

R: Judgmental? All I said was "Don't have a fit about it." Why does that make me judgmental?

B: Having a fit is supposed to be okay?

R: Oh, c'mon, You know what I meant.

B: Yeah. You meant I was unstable.

R: Give me a break, will you?

B: What do you mean, then?

R: Let's stop for a minute.

B: Okay.

R: You were reading this book about Adult Children, and it triggered something that's been gnawing at you. I care about you. I want to know what's gnawing at you.

B: Oh. You really do care, then?

R: Yes, I do.

B: Oh. That feels good. (There is a long silence.) That's what's been gnawing at me. Sometimes we get too far apart and then I wonder if you care about me.

R: I do care about you. And, you know, I agree with you. We do get too far apart sometimes.

B: I feel a lot better. This was beginning to turn into one of those "old-time fights" that we used to have. It was scaring me.

R: I like the way you can identify those subtle feelings. Scared. Yeah. I was scared, too.

B: Thank you. I need some time with you. Without the kids. Without the phone ringing off the hook.

R: I need some time with you, too.

B: When can we get some time like that?

R: I have to get this report done by Monday. But if I got off my rear-end, I could easily get it done by tomorrow night. I've been putting it off because I hate doing it. We could have the whole weekend to ourselves.

B: Where shall we go?

R: Anywhere is fine with me. You pick the spot.

B: I'll do that.

R: I love you.

B: I love you, too.

This interchange began harmlessly, escalated into a near-disaster, and then worked out. There is reciprocity here. Therefore, it works.

But what is reciprocity? Why did it work? It worked because these two people have equal power, need, influence, dependency, independence, interdependence, separateness, strength, courage, dignity, self-respect and ... well

... their cups are relatively full. "The paradox" is not a paradox for this particular couple because they have transcended the paradox. They have gone beyond it. This particular paradox can't hurt them anymore. Not for now, anyway. They've done some work.

Another couple, in a different place in their relationship and growth, have resolved the paradox in another way:

> **D:** I've been reading this book about Adult Children and intimacy, and it says we either get too enmeshed or too detached. What do you think we do?
>
> **L:** I don't know, I'm pretty satisfied with our relationship.
>
> **D:** You know, I guess it's been bothering me lately that we hardly talk to each other anymore. It feels like we've drifted apart awfully far.
>
> **L:** Oh?
>
> **D:** Yes, I feel sort of sad about it.
>
> **L:** I see.
>
> **D:** And I guess if you feel like everything's okay, then we have a problem on our hands.
>
> **L:** There you go again!
>
> **D:** What do you mean?
>
> **L:** You're always harping about how much time we spend together and I think we spend enough time together. Sometimes it's too much.
>
> **D:** I hear ya.
>
> **L:** Good. Then let's just drop it, okay?
>
> **D:** Okay. But before we drop it, I need to decide what I want to do about it. (There is a painfully long silence as "D" checks in with the feelings that are slowly rising to the surface.) I don't want to become a nag but I have certain needs that I don't want to ignore either. I spent too many years ignoring them in the past. From the sound of it, you feel like I'm on the verge of becoming a nag, so I guess that's why I'm feeling sad.
>
> **L:** Why?
>
> **D:** Because the only alternative for me is to change the nature of our relationship. I think we need to separate for a while. That's why I'm sad.
>
> **L:** Separate? Oh, c'mon now. Letting your emotions run away with you again?

D: No. This time I'm letting my emotions speak to me instead of tyrannize me. I want to separate for a while, and I'm sad about this
decision I must make.

L: That's ridiculous. You can't be serious.

D: It's not ridiculous, and I am serious and I am sad.

L: You really mean this, don't you?

D: Yes I do. I care about you a lot, but I have to be in a relationship
that feels right for me. And this doesn't feel right at the moment.
It's not a matter of right or wrong, good or bad. There's no black-
hat-white-hat here. We simply have very different needs.

What "D" has discovered in the process of recovery is that self-
abandonment is too high a price to pay for a relationship. The way in which
"D" handled this problem indicates that "D" has a basic sense of trust (that
things will work out, even though they are painful now); that "D" has a basic
sense of autonomy (that standing alone is okay when one must do it); that
"D" has a basic sense of initiative (to solve problems and make decisions,
including the tough decisions); and that "D" is clearly on the way to having
a clear identity (a sense of self instead of self-abandonment). In expressing
the painful vulnerable feeling of sadness, "D" also demonstrates at the same
time that most admirable of traits, simple dignity.

There are many excellent books on the market dealing with intimacy. We
happen to like and recommend the following: *Becoming Partners: Marriage
and Its Alternatives* (Rogers, 1973), *Struggle For Intimacy* (Woititz, 1985),
Women Who Love Too Much (Norwood, 1985), *Men Who Hate Women And
the Women Who Love Them* (Forward and Torres, 1986) and *Pairing* (Bach
and Deutsch, 1970). Rogers' and Bach's books are especially good in presenting inside views of the intimate struggles that we all have, and much of
their presentation is by example and vignette, which is a powerful way to get
the message across.

Beyond Intimacy

Being human and in recovery has its benefits. We don't have to be perfect anymore, for one thing. We can have a basic sense of trust and still be

comfortable when our mistrust emerges without warning.

Not being perfect is a true joy. We get to be paranoid now and then without beating ourselves up for it, which is a tremendous relief. Think about how much energy it takes to beat yourself up! It makes a heck of a lot more sense to just say "Hey, I'm really upset about this: I wonder what that's about?" Period. End of discussion with self. No guilt, blame, shame or self-destruction. Trust that the answer will come when we least expect it—you know, when we're changing a diaper or balancing the checkbook.

As comedian Steven Wright so wisely said, "You can't have everything. Where would you put it?" It is such an elegant sentiment, and it is wonderfully liberating! Nobody can have it all. If that is truth, then I am now free, because there are five billion people on this planet and not one of them is perfect! So I can trust that I am okay even when I don't trust all the time!

It is the same with autonomy, initiative, industry, identity and intimacy. The building blocks must be fairly solid, but they will never be perfect. If we learn to make friends with the Little Child inside of us; if we learn to listen to our feelings which are felt inside of our bodies; if we are scared and admit that we are scared; if we are angry and admit that we are angry; and if we are open to learning from those who have more wisdom than we do, then we will find what we are searching for on this earth.

And if our building blocks are fairly solid up to and including the intimacy stage, then Erikson feels that our next challenge is . . .

Generativity versus Self-Absorption

Somewhere between our mid-twenties and our mid-thirties or later, depending upon when we get into recovery, we have a crisis that revolves around self versus others. Part of us wants to focus so deeply on the self that we exclude all else. The other part of us wants to start giving back to humanity what was given to us thus far. The dilemma here is that if we haven't got much to begin with (if we are Adult Children who haven't begun a solid recovery program yet; if we were abused as children but haven't admitted it and dealt with it yet; if we are in a "pseudo-recovery" in which we say the right things but don't live them), then we won't have much to give back.

Our generativity will direct us to bear children, but we will unconsciously abuse them the way that we were abused. Our generativity will direct us to create the ultimate work of art, but we will become so absorbed in the process that we will shoot ourselves in the foot while we're trying.

We see many people doing 12th-step work (helping other people to begin recovery programs) as a method of avoiding their own personal issues. Yes, it's true. Helping others can be an excuse for avoiding one's own work and pain. We have done it ourselves, so we know.

Erikson's simple wisdom is that we are not truly ready to give something back to humanity until we have got what we needed as children. For those of us who are psychotherapists, this is evidenced in the statement that "we can only help those who are worse off than we are." All of us run amuck when we focus on generativity before we've done our identity, intimacy and earlier work.

Perhaps the best advice here is to say: *'Tis Better to Give Back from a Full Cup Than From an Empty One.*

Integrity versus Despair

Each stage in our lives brings with it a period of reflection about the past. We do this when we first leave home, then again during our 30s crisis, at the midlife crisis, and so forth. These are all preparation for the *life review* that takes place in old age, when we go back over our entire life and try to make sense out of it. If we can review our life and be left with a sense of wholeness, completion and serenity, then we can face our own death secure in the knowledge that we have lived a full, rich, rewarding life.

Part of this life review process includes looking at past mistakes and regrets, dealing with the loss and sadness that these bring, and finishing up any business with loved ones that has not yet been finished. We may need to apologize to someone. Or we may need to tell someone that their behavior made us angry and we've been carrying around that anger all these years. Or we may simply need to tell someone that we love them and that we appreciate their love.

For those of us who have risked passing through all of the preceding stages of life, old age and death do not have to be awful and frightening. To the contrary, it can be a period of wisdom and wholeness. As Plato wrote in *The Republic*, approximately 370 B.C.: "Old age has a great sense of calm and freedom. When the passions have relaxed their hold, you have escaped, not from one master, but from many."

For those of us who have not taken the risks to have our feelings and live our lives fully, old age can be a terrible curse.

We often recall reading the case study in a psychiatric text about a woman who spent her entire life caring for her hypochondriacal, manipulative mother. The other two children in the family grew up and left home, leaving the youngest in the clutches of Mom. Upon Mom's death at the age of 95, this youngest daughter of hers, now 70 years old, had a complete and total psychotic breakdown, tearing out her hair, slashing her wrists and smashing her head into the wall over and over in a hopeless rage at the fact that she had devoted her *entire* life to someone who was supposed to have let her go free in late adolescence.

Too often we Adult Children are not only victims of our unrecovering parents while we are children, but also when we are adults and our parents are old and dying. And yet, even the most dysfunctional parents can die with a sense of wholeness if they are open to it. Growth here on earth doesn't stop until we die.

We are reminded of a friend of ours whose parents died recently. Both were chemically dependent and "recovering" in old age, primarily because of medical reasons. Both had had tremendous conflicts throughout their 51-year marriage, with the last 10 to 15 years being relatively peaceful. And it was not until the very last year of her life that his mother was able to attain that serenity which is encouraged by all of our 12-step programs. But attain it she did. At her funeral our friend read the following (excerpted from a longer eulogy):

"Mom, your life was a mixture of great joy and deep sorrow. For the joys that you experienced, I am very happy. For the sorrow that you experienced, I am sad now, but that will pass. Sadness allows healing; and I understand that those little deaths along the way give us depth and wisdom. The last year of your life was filled with a serenity that I shall never forget . . . I want to thank you for the tremendous dignity that you demonstrated this past year, in living alone, and in your dying, and also for the wisdom to fight to die in your own house. You went 'gently into that good night,' and I have hope now that I can do the same someday."

We would like to end this chapter with a quote from Charles Dickens:

Father Time is not always a hard parent, and, though he tarries for none of his children, often lays his hand lightly on those who have used him well.

—*Charles Dickens,* Barnaby Rudge, vol. II, 1840

Interlude

15

The Rabbit

Once upon a time not so long ago, a Little Rabbit was born in a burrow along the edge of a beautiful forest. Her mother and father cared for her diligently, and she was growing up healthy and strong.

Then one day as her parents were heading toward the burrow at the end of the day, a fox leaped from behind a tree, chased her mother down, and killed her and ate her. The Little Rabbit's father ran as fast as he could until he got home, where he told the Little Rabbit what had happened. They were both very sad and very afraid, and the father did not leave the burrow for many days.

But they needed to eat, and so one day he left the burrow to look for food. He was very cautious and very nervous. As he was nibbling on some small green plants not more than a few steps from the entrance to the burrow, the wily fox leaped from behind a tree, chased him down and ate him right on the spot. The Little Rabbit was shaking inside the burrow because she knew what had happened. She crawled down as far as she could in the burrow, and cried herself to sleep.

The next morning the Little Rabbit awoke very hungry, but she was afraid to leave the burrow. Then suddenly, from a distance, she could hear the voices of two children who were passing through the forest on their way home. She crawled up to the entrance of the burrow and poked her nose out to sniff the air. There was no sign of the fox, so she peeked out of the burrow to see where the voices were coming from. The two children were walking right toward her burrow, but for some reason the Little Rabbit was not afraid. They looked liked such happy, gentle children.   .

When they got a little closer, they spied the Little Rabbit peeking out of her burrow. They walked a little closer and then sat down to wait for the Little Rabbit to come out. Finally she did.

"How are you, Little Rabbit?" they asked.

"Not very well," replied the Little Rabbit. "My parents have been killed by an evil fox and I am all alone here in my burrow. I am afraid to come out and forage for food, and I fear that I shall starve if I don't eat soon."

"Well," said the children, "why don't you come with us? You can live at our house and we will feed you and keep you safe from all harm."

The Little Rabbit was very happy. She trusted these children, and she said that she would love to live with them. She hopped out of her burrow and jumped into the arms of one of the children, and they took her home. They took very good care of her, and she lived with them for several years.

Then one day she decided to go into the forest to look for some food. While in the forest, she met three other rabbits, who were very excited to introduce themselves to her. They thought that she was very pretty.

"Hello, Little Rabbit," said the first one.

"You are a very pretty rabbit," said the second one.

"Would you like to go for a walk with us?" asked the third.

The Little Rabbit was confused, and then she blurted out, "I *am not a rabbit!*"

The three rabbits looked surprised, and then chuckled loudly to each other.

"If you aren't a rabbit," asked one of them, "then what are you?" "I am a person," she answered angrily.

"A person!" laughed the second rabbit. They fell to the ground and began laughing hysterically.

"Do people have long ears and fur?" asked the third.

"Some of them do," she cried. "I've seen them." The tears began rolling down her face in rivulets. "I am not a rabbit!" she said again. By this time, the three rabbits realized that she was serious. They asked her where she lived and how she found food, and she told them that she lived with the other people in a house not far from where they were in the forest. Before they could ask her anymore questions, she hopped away and went home.

That night, she talked to the two children and told them what had happened. They didn't have the heart to tell her that the three rabbits had been right. And so she went to sleep that night, secure in the reality that she was a person and not a rabbit.

The next day, she went into the forest again. Something told her that she needed to go, but wasn't sure what it was. And so she went despite her doubts. She was in the forest for quite a long time, and a part of her was hoping to see the three rabbits again. After all, they did think that she was pretty, and they had been nice to her aside from their rude laughter. But they were nowhere to be seen. She nibbled on some fresh greens, drank from a babbling brook nearby, and then started home.

After hopping just a few yards, she stopped. Her heart began pounding, and her stomach knotted up. Her breathing became shallow, and she stood still, being very, very quiet. She smelled something ominous. "The fox! Oh, no!" She had never seen a fox, she thought. She didn't even know what a fox was, she thought. Then how could I even say "The Fox," she asked herself. Something strange was happening. And then she saw him. He was not more than 15 yards away, lurking behind a bush, ready to pounce on her and kill her. She was frozen with fear!

A split second before the fox leaped toward her, she spied something out of the corner of her eye. They were three rabbits, dressed in strange costumes and wielding three sharp swords with curved blades, known as scimitars.

A fourth rabbit jumped from behind a tree and shouted, "Here, take this and defend yourself!" He hurled one of the scimitars in her direction, and without thinking, she deftly caught it by the handle and reared up on her hind legs to face the fox.

The fox leaped toward her, mouth drooling and fangs bared. Her heart raced. Images of her dead parents flashed through her mind's eye. The adrenalin coursed through her veins. The fox sailed through the air! She took one step to the side very quickly, disorienting the fox. And then with all the strength she could muster, she made the scimitar do its work. Swoosh! Swoosh! Swoosh! The blade of the scimitar sliced through the air back and forth with graceful power! Whit! Whit! The tip of the blade cut into the fox enough to draw blood but not enough to kill him. Confused and frightened, the fox raced into the woods, where he could be left alone to lick his wounds.

"Three cheers for the Rabbit! Hooray for the Rabbit!" they cheered. Tears welled up in her eyes. They were tears of relief. "I am a Rabbit," she cried, joyfully.

"Hooray! Hooray! Hooray!" cheered the other rabbits. As she turned to thank them, she was amazed at what she saw. Forty rabbits came out from behind all the trees that surrounded her. And then, a forty-first rabbit, dressed more fashionably than the rest, emerged.

"Who are you?" she asked.

The forty-first rabbit answered, "I am Ali Baba. And these are the 40 Robber Rabbits."

"Robber Rabbits?" she asked.

"Well, not really. I mean, we don't rob from just anybody. We help animals in the forest protect themselves from predators. The wolves and foxes called us Robber Rabbits and the name just caught on."

"I see," said the Brave Little Rabbit. And then she said, "I thank you for helping me to save my own life. But even more than that it has helped me to see that indeed I am a Rabbit. And I am proud to be a Rabbit!"

"Three cheers for the Brave Little Rabbit!" shouted Ali Baba and the 40 Robber Rabbits.

"And three cheers for me," thought the Brave Little Rabbit. "Three cheers for me."

Part IV

Beneath the Iceberg

*Whatever is hidden away will be brought out into the open,
and whatever is covered up will be uncovered.*

Mark 4:22

16

A General Model of Adult Children and Co-dependency

We have used the term "co-dependency" a few times thus far. It is likely that many of you who read this book are familiar with the term. Many of you perhaps use the word several times a day. Despite the fact that we are probably best known for our research and clinical work in the area of co-dependency, we felt that it was important to hold off on any discussion of it until this point in the book because there is a lot of confusion surrounding the term. We believe that the term "co-dependency" has been, and still is, in a state of evolution.

Co-dependency originally meant the spouse, lover or significant other of someone who was chemically dependent. At that beginning point in its evolution, it was simple to understand. Whether you had any symptoms yourself or not, if you were involved somehow with a chemically dependent person, then you were a co-dependent.

But since those simpler early days, "co-dependency" has taken on a life and an identity of its own. Many professionals now feel that co-dependency is a specific diagnostic term which refers to a specific set of emotional and behavioral symptoms.

Robert Subby and John Friel defined it as a dysfunctional pattern of living that was learned by a set of rules within the family system (Subby & Friel, 1985). Subby used a similar definition in his recent book entitled *Lost in the Shuffle: The Co-Dependent Reality* (Subby, 1987).

Noted psychiatrist and Chairman of the National Association of Children of Alcoholics Dr. Timmen Cermak makes an excellent case for defining co-dependency as a clear-cut psychiatric disorder in his book *Diagnosing and Treating Co-Dependence* (Cermak, 1986).

Co-dependency Symptoms

In listing the symptoms of co-dependency, we and others most often look at issues such as "caretaking," "over-responsibility" to others and an inability to care for self appropriately, difficulty in identifying and expressing feelings, swinging from "too nice" to angry and abusive, over-focusing on others while under-focusing on self, identity development problems, and getting into abusive and/or confusing relationships.

In co-dependency we do not believe that we have choices, which produces a painful feeling of "stuck-ness." Along with this symptom is a lot of compulsiveness, too. In our seminars we often say, "In our co-dependency we don't know how to start and we don't know how to stop."

Our own work in this area began in 1982 when we likened co-dependency to a "paradoxical dependency" (Friel, 1982) in which we appear strong, competent and emotionally healthy on the outside but feel confused, lost, lonely and dependent on the inside.

This type of co-dependency, of course, is now seen as just one of many forms that the disorder can take, depending upon one's role in their family of origin and upon the stage of co-dependency that one is currently in. The strong, responsible, hold-everything-together type of co-dependency can give way to an abusive, rageful, unpredictable, irresponsible form under certain conditions.

Confusion also develops over the concept because one of the common symptoms of untreated co-dependency is simply chemical dependency. In fact, it has been our clinical experience and that of many other professionals with whom we communicate that most chemically dependent and other addicted people are also co-dependent beneath their addiction.

In 1984, we began presenting a model of co-dependency which has served us very well in our clinical work, and which has been extremely well-received by the professional community and client populations alike. Clients like our definition and "iceberg model" because they make both "intuitive sense" and are easily understandable. The professionals in the fields of mental health, chemical dependency, medicine and law whom we have trained with the model, state that it is also easily understood, as well as clarifying the complex and confusing relationship between chemical addictions, relationship addictions, other addictions and co-dependency. We offer here our definition and conceptual model:

> Co-dependency is a dysfunctional pattern of living that emerges from our family of origin as well as our culture, producing arrested identity development, and resulting in an over-reaction to things outside of us and an under-reaction to things inside of us. Left untreated, it can deteriorate into an addiction.

The *dysfunctional pattern of living* is the symptomology that we have come to identify with being co-dependent, and includes depression, tolerance of inappropriate behavior, dulled or inappropriate affect, self-defeating coping strategies, strong need to control self and others, stress-related physical symptoms, abuse of self, neglect of self, difficulty with intimacy and/or sexuality, fear of abandonment, shame, inappropriate guilt, eventual addictions, rages, etc. In other words, all of the symptoms of Adult Children outlined in Chapter 3.

Where Does Co-dependency Come From?

When we say that co-dependency *emerges from our family of origin*, we are stating clearly that we do not believe that people become co-dependent because they have been living with an addict. Rather, we are stating that they are in relationship with an addict *because* they are co-dependent. Clients who say, "But I didn't know she was an addict when I married her," later discover through their own recovery that they indeed had chosen someone who fit the family-of-origin rules that they themselves had grown up with. In other words, water seeks its own level.

The next part of our definition, *as well as our culture*, means that we believe that our culture has many elements in it that foster and maintain co-dependent behavior patterns, These can include interpretations of religion that are rigid, dogmatic and authoritarian, and in which people are led to believe that they are bad if they ever think of their own needs prior to thinking of someone else's needs.

Other cultural influences are our schools, in which children are too often expected to conform, be "nice" and be so much like each other that they lose their individuality and their ability to question life for themselves. Our American emphasis on technological "cures" and "fixes" for everything can also foster co-dependency because it increases our alienation from ourselves and each other and heightens our fears of abandonment.

The foundation for our definition is the notion of *arrested identity development*. Building on the work of Erik Erikson, we have argued that beneath our adult masks we are actually stuck in pre-adolescent identity formation stages when we have notable co-dependent patterns.

In our pamphlet *Co-dependency and the Search for Identity: A Paradoxical Crisis* (Friel, Subby and Friel, 1985) we likened co-dependency to the foreclosed identity state first proposed by Erikson. Thus, we are like wounded children wearing the masks of adulthood, frightened that someone will "find us out" or expose us for what we truly are—wounded children. Tim Cermak refers to our identity model as one of several major theoretical frameworks for understanding co-dependency in his recent book *Diagnosing and Treating Co-dependency* (1986).

The *over-reaction to things outside of us* is the addictive and the denial part of co-dependency. We can help others in their crises; we can become work-addicted and super-responsible; we can focus on all the negative hurtful things that our alcoholic or addicted spouse/friend does to us; and we can blame others for our misery because these are all ways of avoiding our own internal reality and pain, which leads to the next part of our definition, which is *an under-reaction to things inside of us*. These things that we are avoiding are our feelings, our pain, our joy, hopes and dreams. These things inside of us *are* us. Co-dependency is thus a dangerous denial of self.

A Unifying Model of
Co-dependency and Addictions

Our "iceberg model" that we have been using since 1984 is shown in Figure 16.1. It is borrowed from the psychodynamic notion that what is on the surface (in our model, the more overt symptoms of addiction, depression, stress-disorders, etc.) is tied to a much deeper inner reality of guilt, shame and fear of abandonment, which was learned in our family of origin. Mediating between our surface symptoms and this deeper reality is what we are calling "co-dependency."

Thus, when we begin to remove the alcoholism, sexual addiction, eating/food disorders, migraine headaches or whatever, through primary treatment, what we are left with is our co-dependency. That co-dependency must also be treated if we are to avoid the risk of relapse. Our model also allows for the explanation of the various forms that addiction take and the various roles that we can cycle through, including the "offender," "victim" and "rescuer" roles. Thus, some relationship addicts are victims, some are offenders and some are rescuers, but they are all co-dependent underneath it.

Some alcoholics are terribly irresponsible, some are constant rescuers, and some are constantly being victimized, but we believe that most alcoholics are co-dependent underneath it all.

Co-dependency Roots

In considering biochemical and genetic theories of addiction, we do not deny that some alcoholism, some depression, some obesity, etc., is genetically caused. But we would qualify this and say that a person who is genetically predisposed to become alcoholic will have a much greater chance of actually becoming alcoholic if he or she has a deep foundation of co-dependency learned from their family of origin. Likewise, this addict will be much less likely to achieve quality sobriety as long as the underlying co-dependency is left untreated.

Delving deeper into the iceberg in Figure 16.1, we see that the roots of our co-dependency are guilt, shame, and fear of abandonment (inability to trust), which correspond to Erikson's first three psychosocial crises.

The guilt accounts for our inability to make decisions, to get "unstuck" and to take our own needs into account. It is this guilt that keeps us protecting our family of origin and unable to protect ourselves at the level closest to the surface of ourselves.

Figure 16.1. Unifying Model of Co-dependency and Addictions

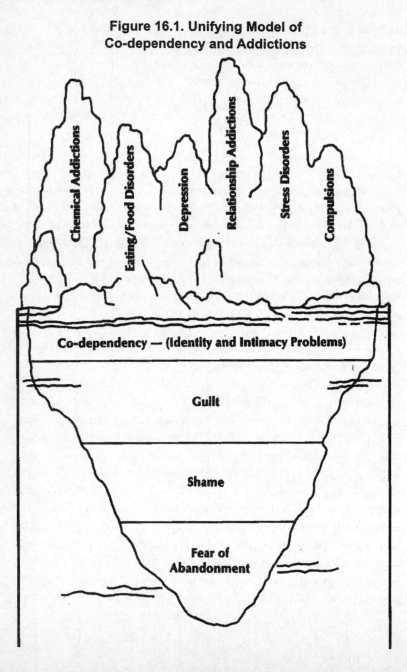

Chemical Addictions

Eating/Food Disorders

Depression

Relationship Addictions

Stress Disorders

Compulsions

Co-dependency — (Identity and Intimacy Problems)

Guilt

Shame

Fear of Abandonment

The shame represents our inability to be separate, to stand alone, to enjoy being alone, to be interdependent with others and to feel good about ourselves. It represents our feelings of being broken and defective—that we don't make mistakes, we are mistakes. The fear of abandonment is at the very core of our being. If we are co-dependent, it means that at a deep, unconscious level, we believe that we do not have the right to exist, to live or to survive. It is there because either literally and overtly, or metaphorically and covertly, we were abandoned or neglected over and over again in our childhoods, until our trust was so eroded that we couldn't trust anyone.

Is Co-dependency Universal?

Given our definition, it is not true that almost everyone is co-dependent? Is it not true that almost everyone had some form of dysfunction in their childhood that could lead to co-dependent symptoms? And if everyone has "it," does it not lose its conceptual and diagnostic meaning? We think not, for the same reasons that "depression" has not lost its meaning despite the fact that everyone has "it" sometimes. The Diagnostic and Statistical Manual of the American Psychiatric Association (DSM-III-R) always describes symptoms, but asks us to look at length and severity of symptoms, as well as total number of symptoms, before we make a definite diagnosis. The same should be true with co-dependency. Just because everyone has some co-dependent behavior does not mean that the concept is therefore useless.

One of the major criticisms of "co-dependency," at least in Minnesota, is that it is discriminatory toward women because our culture encourages women to practice some co-dependent behaviors as part of their "normal" female role. Our definition and model of co-dependency does not fall into this trap, we believe, because it is neither "male" nor "female" in bias. It implies that too much focus on others is unhealthy, as is too little focus on others. It allows for separate male and female identities and, like recent models of psychological androgyny, presumes that the healthiest of us are able to apply both male and female traits where and when appropriate. It also implies that victim behavior is unhealthy whether in a man or woman, as is offender behavior or rescuer behavior. Thus, it avoids what we believe has become a dangerous and false dichotomy, and a misleading stereotype, of the "abusive-offender-male-addict-married-to-the-overly-responsible-saint-of-a-Mom-co-dependent-victim-rescuer."

In other words, we see co-dependency resulting from abuse and neglect in childhood. Some co-dependents later go on to medicate the pain of their co-dependency by becoming alcoholic or drug addicted. Others handle that pain by becoming saints or martyrs. Others become workaholic, compulsive housecleaners, addicted to their children, to television, to relationships, etc. Some manipulate, some are manipulated, and most do both in cycles.

Treatment Implications

Our model also has some clear implications for treatment. We generally agree with the need to treat the overt addiction first because it is that addiction which prevents us from having our feelings and from admitting our underlying co-dependency.

If it *is* a relationship addiction, we need to stop practicing the relationship, just as we would have to stop using chemicals in the case of a chemical addiction. So primary treatment of the major surface symptom should come first.

The next step in recovery is to identify the underlying co-dependency issues. These will be primary issues of identity and identity formation, which ultimately require that one goes deep inside oneself, one's past and one's family of origin to deal with the issues of guilt, shame and fear of abandonment. This is an intrapsychic as well as a family systems task, and it cannot be done overnight in a 30-day treatment program for co-dependency. It can be begun in such a program, but requires a recovery process of 12-step support in A.A., Al-Anon, Adult Children of Alcoholics or Co-dependents Anonymous. Individual psychotherapy is needed, plus intensive group psychotherapy for shame reduction.

As far as recovery is concerned, a good gauge of how well we are doing is to notice when we stop saying, "How long will it take before I recover from this pain?" The less we say this, the closer we are getting to recovery. Because healthy life, we feel, is pain and joy and sadness and anger and confusion and happiness and loneliness and warmth and closeness and ... Recovery means reaching deep inside to that wounded child so that he or she can begin to heal from the inside out. And that usually takes years, and is worth every minute of it.

Assessing Co-dependency

To help in identifying the issues of Adult Children and co-dependency discussed thus far, we designed an inventory that we have been using for the past five years, both in research and clinical work. We also find that it is a useful tool for people to begin identifying for themselves the problems that they need to work on.

The Friel Adult Child/Co-dependency Inventory (Friel, 1985) is based on our developmental framework and includes many of the core symptoms which we believe define co-dependency. If you decide to answer the questions in the Inventory, we ask (1) that you answer as honestly as you can, with as much of your own denial put aside as is possible for you at this time; and (2) that you fill it out alone and don't feel that you have to share the results with anyone but yourself. It is very important that you begin focusing on yourself without worrying that anyone else is going to "find you out" or shame you.

To score the inventory, give yourself 1 point for every *"true"* response to all of the *even-numbered* items; and give yourself 1 point for every *"false"* response to the *odd-numbered* items. You can have a possible total score of 60.

In our research thus far, we have found scores from 10 to 20 to indicate mild co-dependency/adult child concerns; scores from 21 to 30 to be in the mild-moderate range; 31 to 45 to be moderate-severe and over 45 to be severe. Rather than keeping score, though, we suggest again that you use this inventory as a means for self-exploration. And as we will discuss in the next chapter, we invite you to arrange for a one-session evaluation with a professional if you feel that you have some of these issues interfering with your happiness and sense of well being.

Friel Adult Child/Co-dependency Assessment Inventory

Below are a number of questions dealing with how you feel about yourself, your life and those around you. As you answer each question, be sure to answer honestly, but do not spend too much time dwelling on any one question. There are no right or wrong answers. Take each question as it comes and answer as you usually feel.

1. I make enough time to do things just for myself each week.
2. I spend lots of time criticizing myself after an interaction with someone.
3. I would not be embarrassed if people knew certain things about me.
4. Sometimes I feel like I just waste a lot of time and don't get anywhere.
5. I take good enough care of myself.
6. It is usually best not to tell someone they bother you; it only causes fights and gets everyone upset.
7. I am happy about the way my family communicated when I was growing up.
8. Sometimes I don't know how I really feel.
9. I am very satisfied with my intimate love life.
10. I've been feeling tired lately.
11. When I was growing up, my family liked to talk openly about problems.
12. I often look happy when I am sad or angry.
13. I am satisfied with the number and kind of relationships I have in my life.
14. Even if I had the time and money to do it, I would feel uncomfortable taking a vacation by myself.
15. I have enough help with everything that I must do each day.
16. I wish that I could accomplish a lot more than I do now.
17. My family taught me to express feelings and affection openly when I was growing up.
18. It is hard for me to talk to someone in authority (boss, teachers, etc.).
19. When I am In a relationship that becomes too confusing and complicated, I have no trouble getting out of it.
20. I sometimes feel pretty confused about who I am and where I want to go with my life.
21. I am satisfied with the way that I take care of my own needs.
22. I am not satisfied with my career.
23. I usually handle my problems calmly and directly.
24. I hold back my feelings much of the time because I don't want to hurt other people or have them think less of me.
25. I don't feel like I'm "in a rut" very often.
26. I am not satisfied with my friendships.
27. When someone hurts my feelings or does something that I don't like, I have little difficulty telling them about it.
28. When a close friend or relative asks for my help more than I'd like, I usually say "yes" anyway.

Friel Adult Child/Co-dependency Assessment Inventory
(cont'd)

29. I love to face new problems and am good at finding solutions to them.
30. I do not feel good about my childhood.
31. I am not concerned about my health a lot.
32. I often feel like no one really knows me.
33. I feel calm and peaceful most of the time.
34. I find it difficult to ask for what I want.
35. I don't let people take advantage of me more than I'd like.
36. I am dissatisfied with at least one of my close relationships.
37. I make major decisions quite easily.
38. I don't trust myself in new situations as much as I'd like.
39. I am very good at knowing when to speak up and when to go along with others' wishes.
40. I wish I had more time away from my work.
41. I am as spontaneous as I'd like to be.
42. Being alone is a problem for me.
43. When someone I love is bothering me, I have no problem telling them so.
44. I often have so many things going on at once that I'm really not doing justice to any one of them.
45. I am very comfortable letting others into my life and revealing "the real me" to them.
46. I apologize to others too much for what I do or say.
47. I have no problem telling people when I am angry with them.
48. There's so much to do and not enough time. Sometimes I'd like to leave it all behind me.
49. I have few regrets about what I have done with my life.
50. I tend to think of others more than I do of myself.
51. More often than not, my life has gone the way that I wanted it to.
52. People admire me because I'm so understanding of others, even when they do something that annoys me.
53. I am comfortable with my own sexuality.
54. I sometimes feel embarrassed by behaviors of those close to me.
55. The important people in my life know "the real me," and I am okay with them knowing.
56. I do my share of work, and often do quite a bit more.
57. I do not feel that everything would fall apart without my efforts and attention.
58. I do too much for other people and then later wonder why I did so.
59. I am happy about the way my family coped with problems when I was growing up.
60. I wish that I had more people to do things with.

Part V

Recovering: What Do I Do Now?

The man of true greatness never loses his child's heart.

Mencius: Discourses, *IV, Circa 300 B.C.*

17

Uncovering
and Admitting

We remember the days before Kenneth Cooper developed his well-known point system for figuring out how much aerobic exercise we get for jogging, swimming and what not (Cooper, 1970). It was great. We could go out on a cool Sunday afternoon in the autumn, run around the block a few times until we worked up a sweat and felt winded, and then return to the comfort of our cozy homes assured that we were doing our bodies wonders by our Herculean efforts. We even bragged about it the next day at work.

"Boy, I feel great! Ran a couple of miles yesterday!" Our colleagues would shake their heads in wonder and chalk it up to second childhood or the onset of early senescence.

But in his sincere and well intentioned way, Kenneth Cooper changed all that. All of a sudden there was an easy-to-understand, foolproof way to determine how much cardiovascular benefit we were really getting from those jogs around the block. A certain number of points for running a mile in eight minutes, and a certain number of points needed each week to maintain good cardiovascular fitness. No ifs, ands or buts.

In confidence, we got in our cars and measured how far we'd been running. Surprise! "Nine tenths of a mile?" we cried in disbelief. "Hell, there must be something wrong with this damned odometer. I'll measure it with the other car." Nine-tenths of a mile it is. "Okay. I'm game. I'll measure out one honest mile and then I'll time myself. I just know I'm in good shape!"

The next day we ran that mile, pushing as hard as we could. Exhausted and on the verge of cardiac arrest, we looked pleadingly at our spouse, stopwatch in hand.

"Well, how'd I do?" we asked.

"Not bad for someone in middle age," came the reply. "Eight-and-a-half minutes."

Eight-and-a-half minutes? And I have to do this how many days a week to maintain cardiovascular fitness? Baloney! Cooper must have figured his tables wrong.

Kenneth Cooper hadn't figured his tables wrong. True, he has adjusted and refined them over the years, but his basic system is not only still intact, but it started and has maintained one of the truly healthy revolutions in America. By breaking our denial system about how much exercise we were really getting, and by introducing a healthy, gradual, sane approach to working up to a regular aerobic exercise program, Kenneth Cooper led literally millions of flabby, short-winded Americans out of the dark ages and into physical fitness.

Yes, it also led many Americans to early heart attack and death; and others into a running addiction that has left them with shin splints, funnylooking disfigured feet and marital breakups, to name a few. We are not skirting the issue of running addictions here just because we are using Cooper's system as an example. Every new technology or system or scientific discovery is open to abuse by human beings. That is as true of the information that we offer you in this book as it is of any other information or machine. In fact, *the inability to use new information or technology in healthy ways is a key symptom of the dysfunction in us*. Our point is that there is a first step that we must take if we are to begin our recovery as Adult Children. We call this step uncovering and admitting.

Uncovering and Admitting

Uncovering and *admitting* are two of the most courageous, painfully honest and supremely growth-enhancing acts that we as human beings can do.

Above all else, *uncovering* and *admitting* require strength, clarity of mind and purpose, trust in oneself and others and faith that the world is basically a decent place in which to be. Because of this, *uncovering* and *admitting* are far removed from the "easy," ordinary things that we do each day. In truth, a very complex series of events, both within ourselves and outside of us, actually precede what we call true *uncovering* and *admitting*.

What Kenneth Cooper did for aerobic exercise was to provide a means for us to *gently erode our denial system* about the true amount of exercise that we were getting. We use the terms "gently erode" because that's exactly what must happen. In all but the most extreme cases, our denial systems break apart *slowly* and *carefully over time* because we have them for a reason that initially made a lot of sense when we built them. Denial systems are built for a logical, sensible purpose. Without them we would be in a lot of trouble psychologically. The real problem arises when that protective denial system that we once built for a good reason begins to get in the way.

If you grew up in an alcoholic family, for example, then it was a normal protective maneuver for you to unconsciously learn to deny your own true feelings because the family messages you received about those feelings were so crazy. The denial of feelings became an absolute survival response for you as a powerless child in an overwhelmingly mixed-up family.

The problem pops up when you become an adult and try to have a family of your own, or when you try to be happy and spontaneous. Then the denial system that you spent so many years developing and refining gets in the way. You might go from one "crazy" relationship to the next. You find yourself in a circle of friends who lean on you all the time but who never seem to let you lean on them. Or when they let you, things get more muddled than ever.

You marry and have children, thinking that all you have to do is marry and have children and you'll be able to "right" all the wrongs that were done to you as a child. Yet you find yourself doing some of the same crazy stuff— screaming at the kids for just being kids, being overly critical and perfectionistic just like Mom or Dad—and wondering why the hell you're doing it when you swore things would never be like that for your children.

Sooner or later, but inevitably nonetheless, you get depressed, tired, worried, anxious and desperate; and still, nothing makes sense. What you're experiencing as a result of growing up in that alcoholic family is the end result of your denial system that protected you so well as a child. And our point here is that what took year after careful year of unconscious building for our own survival will not come tumbling down overnight in a flash of insight with trumpets and angels in the background. It may seem like that for some of us when we finally do break through, but in fact our first breakthrough is actually the result of perhaps years of internal struggle that only now is becoming external.

Those of you who have been fortunate enough to seek help already for these problems will most likely be very familiar with what we have to say. For those of you who have not, we hope that you get something helpful out of it—if only a chance to take some time to think about yourself for a while, instead of always being caught up in the hustle and bustle of daily living.

1. **The first step** in uncovering and admitting is to step back from your life for a healthy chunk of time and just look at it as if you were someone else. This cannot usually be done while you're in the middle of your normal daily routine, so we don't suggest that you try. We have provided an excellent system for looking at one's life in our pamphlet entitled *Life On My Own Terms: Stress Addiction Recovery Guide* (Friel & Friel, 1986).

   If you find that you don't have any time to be alone to do this, then there's already a very good chance that you have a real problem in one of these areas.

   Step back from your life and paint a picture in your mind of what it looks like and feels like. Is it a good life? Does it feel whole? Fulfilling? Warm? Is it what you thought it would be cracked up to be? Is it challenging in a good sort of way, or is it something else? Boring? Too exciting for you to really handle comfortably? Stifling? Scary? Who is in it? Are there enough people in it? Too many? Are they the kind of people you really want to have in it? After all, it's your life, not somebody else's. Do you like them? Do they like you? Remember, you are doing this for you, not for anyone else. Also, remember that our feelings are in a very real sense who we are.

2. **The second step** is to start talking to people about yourself. Get some feedback from your spouse and/or friends. Find out if the way you see things is the same as the way others see them. It is not necessary that we all see things the same, but emotional isolation, whether we are surrounded by people or all alone, is one of the key features of the painful lifestyle of Adult Children.

Does your spouse feel that you are a workaholic? If so, what about your boss? What about your friends? In fact, do you have anyone other than your spouse that you can talk about "personal things" with? If not, then you can be almost 100% sure that you have a problem. Remember that our symptoms and our dysfunction are borne out of shame and the fear of being "discovered," and that healthy people do have people in whom they can confide.

3. **The third step** in uncovering and admitting is to get information. At first, this will only be through reading books like the one you are reading now. And perhaps attending a seminar or workshop in your area on Adult Children, Co-dependency or Addictions. This is a safe way to "test the waters" without having to disclose anything about yourself. You might also want to take our Adult Child/Co-dependency Inventory, or one of the many brief questionnaires published in popular magazines or provided by treatment centers, covering issues such as chemical dependency, eating disorders, sexual addiction, depression, and the like. If you suspect that you might have an addiction, go back to Chapter 4 and ask yourself how many of those characteristics you have. It only takes two or three of those warning signs to warrant having a professional evaluation.

4. **At the fourth** step in this process, you will be making a decision about your current lifestyle and your past. This decision will not come all at once. You may go in and out of believing that you are an Adult Child of a Dysfunctional Family. In fact, we have seen many people actually go through a formal treatment program for an addiction, co-dependency or some other symptom and then return to their denial months later. The A.A. advice to take it "One Day at a Time" is sage advice, because recovery is a process, and part of recovery is admitting to yourself each day that you are an Adult Child.

In summing up this first crucial step in recovery, remember that *uncovering* and *admitting* is itself a process. It is very common for people to get an initial burst of "recovery" in which their defenses come down and they hurt enough to say, "Yes, I am an alcoholic," or "Yes, I came from a dysfunctional family." This burst of insight will often be followed by positive actions such as joining a 12-step program group, getting into therapy or even going to inpatient treatment. But recovery must be lived a day at a time; and the pull of our past and our family systems is strong. If indeed we are alcoholic, sexually addicted, bulimic or chronically depressed (due to our family systems), etc., there will be tremendous pressure from forces within us and outside of us to go back to our old lifestyle.

The glow can wear off. It is pretty easy not to drink while we are in in-patient treatment for alcoholism. It is part of recovery not to drink after we leave treatment. It is also part of recovery for many of us to "test the limits" of the new system.

"I'm not really an alcoholic," we tell ourselves. "I got a great deal out of treatment. It helped me see how my life and my family is dysfunctional. But I'm not really an alcoholic. I just drank because of all the stress." In a few cases we have seen, this is actually true. In the majority, this is simply our denial taking hold of us again. It usually happens when we stop "working our program" of recovery. We stop going to meetings because we get "too busy". Or we stop "checking in with our feelings" each day. Or we get into yet another addictive relationship that is a re-enactment of our original dysfunctional family system. And within only a few days or weeks, we are right back into the isolation, despair, addiction, depression, negative thinking and shame that led us to recovery in the first place.

We believe that life tells us what we need to know about ourselves if we will only listen carefully. We also believe that whatever we need to make it on this earth is always available to us when we are open to it. So even if we slip back into denial and lose everything that is important to us (spouse, family, friends, job, values, meaning), we can get it all back (in a different form, perhaps) if we are again willing to admit that we are powerless over the demons in our lives and are willing to ask for help. *Help is always there if we can take this first step.*

18

Working a Program

In 12-step circles "working a program" means sticking to a daily program of recovery. For those of you not familiar with "12-step programs," we are referring to the original 12 steps of Alcoholics Anonymous, upon which almost all other Anonymous groups have been modeled. But before we speak directly to the issue of recovery, we would like to share with you a typical recovery history.

Jack's Recovery Process

Jack grew up in a middle-class suburban home outside of Denver, Colorado. He is the oldest of three children. He earned a bachelor's degree in business and management in 1969 and then took a job with a local manufacturing firm. Three years after graduation, he married Betsy, and they started a family immediately.

Seven years into the marriage, Jack started feeling "stale." One day a friend from work invited him to go jogging. He agreed, hoping it might help pull him out of the doldrums. It did. Within a few months, Jack had worked up to running 10 miles a day, and by the end of his first year, he ran a marathon. His productivity at work had increased ten-fold and he had renewed vigor and enthusiasm for life. Everyone outside of his home saw him as a ball of fire. He was exciting to be around, was a go-getter at work, was generous and charming.

At the same time that all of this was going on away from home, things within the home began to deteriorate. Betsy and Jack had grown distant from each other. She started to complain to Jack a lot about his long absences from the children and her while he was training for marathons. They would fight for a few hours and then remain cold and aloof for several days.

The children picked up very quickly on this covert tension and started "tip-toeing" around the house during the long periods of silence. Jack and Betsy's sex life all but vanished. Beneath the excitement of his outer life there developed a deep numbness inside of him. Simply sitting down to dinner with Betsy and the kids became a cue for his wanting to escape—to run away from it all. He was bored with the idle chatter that happens at mealtimes. The little day-to-day things that were shared with each other irritated him. He lost interest in his children and his wife.

Roughly two years into this phase of his life, Jack started gambling. At first he just bought a few lottery tickets but the rush of excitement soon overwhelmed him. He escalated to making several trips a year to Reno, where he began losing large sums of money. And towards the end he was taking incredible risks in the stock market.

Betsy thought it was fun at first. She would never have taken the little risks that they were taking all by herself. She even bought a few lottery tickets on her own. But it wasn't fun for long. She lost count of the sleepless nights she spent worrying when "the big loss" would hit and they would be bankrupt. She was absolutely alone, even when Jack was not out gambling, because he was always preoccupied with it. It became a nightmare for her. She finally became too numb to care. Jack had become numb, too, without even knowing it. His entire life consisted of work, running and gambling. He had become completely isolated from his family, his friends and from himself. His three addictions had a stranglehold on him.

Jack's recovery did not come easy. The family therapist that Betsy finally went to recommended that she start going to Adult Children of Alcoholics 12-step groups because her father was an alcoholic. The therapist also recommended that Jack enter inpatient treatment for his gambling addiction. Jack refused.

"This is not a big deal," he proclaimed. "I can deal with it by myself."

But Betsy did not give in. She told him that he would have to become involved in some kind of group therapy experience or she would ask him to move out.

Jack's strategy was to shop around town until he could find a therapist who would see things his way. The first two that he saw recommended treatment. The third said that he should join a men's therapy group, and that he probably wasn't gambling addicted. So he joined that group.

Jack stayed with the group several months, and nothing really changed. But Betsy was changing.

Four months into her therapy, Betsy attended an intensive short-term treatment program for Adult Child/Co-dependency issues. She did a lot of painful work around her family of origin and abuse and neglect issues. She emerged from that program somewhat "raw" but deeply connected to the Little Child inside of her for the first time in her life.

At last a clear picture of her life was emerging for Betsy. She was not satisfied with being the wife of an unrecovering addict. Two months after her short-term treatment experience, Betsy approached Jack calmly but purposefully.

"Jack, I care about you. We have shared a lot of our lives with each other. Because I love you, I can no longer watch and be a part of your self-destruction. I have made a decision that I will stay in this marriage for now if you go to inpatient treatment for gambling addiction. All I know for sure is that I can't live this way anymore." And then she cried honest, unashamed tears.

Jack did go into treatment. It was the most painful thing that he had ever done, because it revealed all of the pain that he had experienced as a child growing up in a dysfunctional family system. He felt renewed and invigorated, though. He had some new hope. He learned quickly that treatment is just the beginning of recovery. He learned that he would always be recovering, rather than recovered. He learned that each day was new; and that each day offered the choice of being in recovery or of acting-out his addiction. He learned that he had work and running addictions, too, and that he would need to deal with those more as time passed and as his spirit healed. He had a few "slips" his first year, when he would buy lottery tickets, but he also kept going to his aftercare therapy group, honestly working his program and he kept attending a Gamblers

Anonymous 12-step group. And he kept getting healthier.

The first two years following Jack's treatment were rough ones for Jack and Betsy. They had never been truly intimate before so they had a lot of learning to do. They became involved in couples' therapy after a while to begin to learn how to share feelings with each other, resolve conflicts without hurting each other irreparably, and to learn how to get their needs met in non-addictive, non-controlling ways.

Five years later Jack and Betsy have a marriage that is working. They still have fights, but the fights get resolved. They still slip into personal isolation, but they see it and do something about it before it becomes serious. They still deny their true feelings at times, but they are so well connected in the recovering community that it is much easier to get back to that Little Child inside of them. They have friends with whom they have shared their struggles. They can laugh and cry together without getting enmeshed in each other's feelings. And they both enjoy immensely the idle chatter that they and their children share at mealtimes.

The Process of Recovering

There are some basic principles of recovering from Adult Child issues that we would like to outline, with the understanding that each person finds recovery in his or her own time and by his or her own means. This does not mean that we can recover alone! People who "recover" alone, by quitting drinking on their own, for example, are not in recovery. Recovery is much more than simply not drinking or not binging and purging food. For many alcoholics, not drinking is relatively easy when compared to the task of living a balanced, healthy life. Recovery is much more about dealing with our underlying co-dependency, guilt, shame and fear-of-abandonment issues. It is about not replacing one symptom with another. It is about not trying to control those around us. It is about having and trusting our feelings and of getting our emotional needs met in healthy ways. It is about feeling like we belong; that we are not better or worse than others. It is about feeling that the world is basically a safe place to be, and that we are okay in the world. Remember these points as you read through the principles of recovery on next page.

1. Recovery is a Process

This is so simple that it borders on being trite; but it is so easy to forget that we must remind ourselves of this principle from time to time. It is easy to feel great when things are going great for us. But when things are not so great, it is crucial to remember that we are on a journey of recovery, which includes ups and downs. Life presents us with stress and tragedy, whether we are bulimics or not. Life is unpredictable whether we are compulsive overeaters or not. Life is hard sometimes whether we are Adult Children or not.

2. Recovery Cannot Be Done Alone

As we have said many times already, trying to do it alone is one of the primary symptoms of our dysfunction. This has a lot to do with the core shame from our childhoods. We don't want others to know what is going on inside of us because we are afraid that they will be shocked, will reject or abandon us or shame us further. It also has to do with our need to be in control in unhealthy ways. It has to do with the arrogance and moral superiority that is such a strong part of co-dependency.

"She's the addict," we spout. "When she starts recovering, my life will be fine." Translated, this means: "I am better than her." Unfortunately, this feeling of "better than" also leaves plenty of room for feeling "worse than" others, which leads to social and emotional isolation.

Recovery cannot be done alone because the experience of sharing our inner selves with others in a safe way is what we have been missing all our lives. True, we may have lots of people with whom we share our problems late into the night, but are they people who don't get enmeshed with us? Are they people who let us have our pain so that we can learn from it and do something about it, or do they enable us, and get secret satisfaction out of feeling that they are better than us? Do they need to be needed, or can they simply be there for us without trying to "fix" us and offer solutions all the time?

We cannot recover alone but we also cannot recover if all of our time is spent with others who are not in recovery either.

3. Recovery is Painful

This is what keeps so many of us away from recovery. "It has to get worse before it gets better" is one of the key principles of therapy. Digging back

into an abusive and neglectful childhood is not easy or fun. Letting down
our defenses and feeling the deep pain inside of that Little Child locked up
in us hurts. Cleaning out an infection with a scalpel hurts more than the infection, but it is often the only way to heal once and for all. We do not ad-
vocate a life of constant pain or martyrdom, but we do know that this pain
of recovery must happen. And when it does, this pain will eventually subside.

4. Recovery Means Changes In How We Feel, How We Act And In What We Believe

It is not enough to just "think our way through it." It is not enough to just
"feel our way through it." It is not enough to just "act our way through it."
Some of us are great at reading and thinking about recovery and so we tend
to get stuck here. Others are great at expressing certain feelings, and this is
where we get stuck. Still others of us are very adept at changing our behavior to fit what others expect of us. Recovery means making changes in all
three areas, and in achieving a healthy measure of congruence among all
three. That is, what we do is consistent with how we feel, which is consistent with what we believe about ourselves and the world.

5. Recovery Means Getting Out Of Our Roles

In Chapter 6 we discussed some of the dysfunctional roles that we get
caught up in as we are growing up in our families. We noted that these roles
are distorted mutations of truly healthy needs that we have. Recovery means
giving up the role of mascot, hero, princess, enabler, and so on, and getting
those same needs met in healthy ways.

The family caretaker, for example, will feel tremendous guilt at first when
he chooses to no longer take care of Mom's feelings or Dad's alcoholism.
But the more a caretaker is able to give up this role, the more he or she will
be able to have healthy mutuality in all relationships. Likewise, we must give
up the roles of offender, victim and rescuer, breaking the vicious cycle that
happens with these three roles.

6. In Recovery, We Recover Our Choices

This is so hard for us to grasp at first. Time and again our clients will
state that they have no choices. This is experienced as the powerful feeling
of being stuck, which is a key symptom of co-dependency. In our co-

dependency traps, we become reactors to people and events around us, never realizing that we can choose and take action. Because of our dysfunctional belief systems, we paint ourselves into a corner where we are miserable but see no way out. This is one reason that we believe that family-of-origin therapy is essential to recovery, because it is those distorted childhood beliefs that keep us painted in that corner.

"If I tell him that I feel he has a cocaine addiction, he'll just leave me. If he leaves me, I will be alone. If I am left alone, I will not be able to survive. If I cannot survive, I will die. Furthermore, a good wife always stays with her husband no matter what. That's what our marriage vows say. If I confront his cocaine addiction, I am being a bad wife because I will be causing the end of our marriage." This is the kind of logic that we use to keep ourselves stuck.

At some point in the recovery process we will be able to say, "I have recovered my choices."

7. Recovery Requires Transcending Paradoxes

A paradox is something that appears to be contradictory but in fact is true. It is essential in recovery that we let go of black-and-white thinking, which is at the root of these paradoxes in which we get trapped.

For example, can someone be "good" and "bad"? Can we love and hate the same person? Can we become powerful by "giving in"? The answer to all of these questions is "yes." Yet, before recovery, we struggle very hard with these questions. We want to label him "good" and her "safe," when in fact it is humanly impossible for anyone to be "good" all the time or always "safe" to be with. Likewise, love and hate are not opposites, in our opinion. The opposite of love is indifference.

As Confucius wrote many centuries ago, "Only the truly kind man knows how to love and how to hate."

In Summary

The basic elements of any recovery program will include one and usually more of the following:

1. Regular participation in an ongoing 12-step, self-help group is a must. We always require this. (See the Appendix for a list of 12-step groups.)
2. Individual psychotherapy.
3. Group psychotherapy.

4. Family therapy.
5. Inpatient or outpatient treatment.

If the dysfunction that we experienced in our childhoods was mild, participation in a 12-step group may be sufficient. The bottom line will always be the quality of life that we are experiencing (we do not mean the financial quality of life, by the way).

Oftentimes people will expend a lot of time and energy in therapy during the first two years of recovery. They will then reach a point of new-found stability and then just maintain their recovery with a self-help support group. Then as life progresses and becomes richer, there may be a need to delve even deeper into issues that have not yet been addressed.

A large precentage of women who attend inpatient treatment for chemical dependency are survivors of incest or sexual abuse, for example. The first two years of recovery may be just about the chemical addiction—quitting the use of chemicals, changing friendship patterns to others who are also in recovery, and so on. Later on, it will be necessary to address the sexual abuse issues in therapy but only when one is ready to do so.

We have summarized the recovery process in the following flow chart. (See Figure 18.1.)

Recovery is lifelong, and it becomes less and less painful as we progress. Stresses that five years ago would have thrown us into a deep depression are now handled directly with strength and wisdom. Stresses that put us on the verge of acting out our symptoms now, will not do so five years from now. It is not life that changes. It is we who change.

Recovery is a relearning process in which, step by step, we come to see and feel and know the Little Child inside of us.

Recovery is allowing ourselves to experience the truth. At first, this is terribly painful. In the end, it lets us make that Child inside of us feel safe, warm, lovable, whole, proud, honest, peaceful and real.

Figure 18.1. Recovery Process Flow Chart

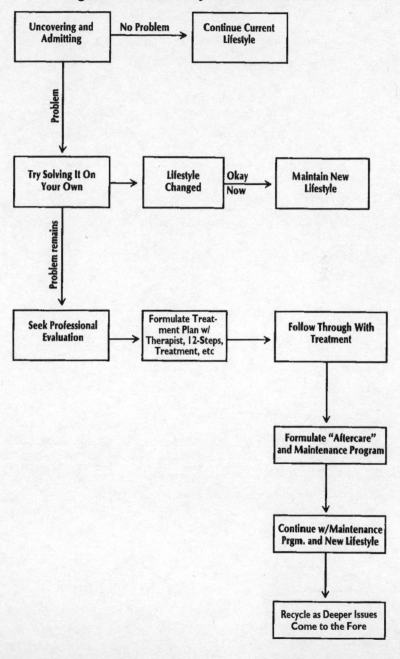

19

A Word about Healing and Spirituality

All Adult Children and Co-dependents are victims of abuse and neglect. The core inside of us has been damaged. We have called this core inside of us our Little Child. What needs to heal are the *guilt, shame* and *fear of abandonment* experienced in our Little Child. Ultimately, our healing must take place from the inside out.

In Chapter 3 we talked about our symptoms as being about feelings and about intimacy. Put another way, our symptoms block relationship. They block our relationship with ourself; they block our relationship with others; they block our relationship with the world at large and they block our relationship with our own spirituality. The only way to truly heal, then, is to restore our ability to be in relationship. This is why recovery never happens alone. It is a contradiction in terms.

"Spirituality" itself is cause for much controversy and inner battling for so many of us. The idea of a Higher Power, which is an essential part of 12-step recovery programs, keeps many people away from Anonymous groups for a long time.

185

"I don't want any of that 'God stuff,'" we proclaim loudly. "I've had it up to here with that."

The authors believe this is true because spirituality is misunderstood. We believe that many of us confuse spirituality with formal religion. Part of it gets confused because somewhere along the line we were presented with a lot of black-and-white thinking—you must either be a Catholic, a Protestant, a Jew, a Buddhist, a Moslem, or you are nothing at all. This puts our Little Child in a double bind which makes us want to avoid the issue altogether. So we want to make it very clear that we are talking about spirituality, *not* religion. The religion you choose or don't choose is your own business, not ours.

As we view it, *spirituality is one's relationship with the unexplainable,* ineffable, the vastness and power of the universe. Some of us call this entity God; others do not. Our spirituality is what allows us to let go of things over which we have no true control, such as other people, other people's feelings and love or lack of it, accidents, tragedies or death itself. Our spirituality allows us to trust that our lives will make sense and that there is a purpose to life, which we will discover, paradoxically, if we stop fighting so hard to find it.

If you have ever stood on the top of a mountain or at the edge of the sea and experienced a tremendous feeling of power and connectedness with the universe, while at the same time, experiencing a feeling of incredible smallness and personal insignificance, then you have had a taste of spirituality. It is frightening and incredibly energizing at the same time.

But spirituality is more than just these momentary feelings that we have when we commune with nature. It is a feeling of connectedness with the entire human race—with all those who have gone before us and all those who will come after us. From there, it is the ultimate relationship with all of creation that becomes our highest form of spirituality.

Imagine what happens to one's relationship with something more powerful or unexplainable than oneself, when he or she is the victim of abuse and neglect. The first "higher power" (metaphorically speaking) that we experience in life are those who raise us from infancy—usually our parents. If those parents abuse us and neglect us, they will be teaching us not to trust entities more powerful than ourselves. We will always be fearful of people in authority. We will constantly defend against the unexplainable. We will seek comfort by trying to control everything around us so that we don't get hurt again. And we will be destined to fail, because we are not gods, and we can never control everything around us.

In our fear and in our damage, we will try nevertheless. In other words, we will try to become our own gods. This is why so many of us turn to chemical addictions—because chemicals give us the illusion that we are in control of it all and because they let us feel connected to the universe for a while, at least until the drug wears off. It is our spirituality that is perhaps the last part of us that is reclaimed after we get into recovery. And it, too, comes back in steps and stages.

Recovery of our spirituality begins when we are truly able to say that we are powerless over our addictions, symptoms or our family systems. The paradox here is that at the very moment that we *surrender*, we gain back some of our true power. Rather than being left *more* vulnerable and defenseless by this surrender, we actually become *less* vulnerable, because now we are not operating according to a self-defeating, destructive logic that depletes all of our energies trying to control things over which we have no control. We are also less vulnerable because we are living in truth and reality instead of in denial and defensiveness. Without the denial, we can use that energy to make positive decisions about our life in areas in which we do have a choice.

After this surrender, we are then able to trust others just a little bit, which begins to restore our relationship with other human beings. For many people, their "higher power" is initially the members of their recovery group.

As we experience sharing our Little Child with others in a safe setting, we realize that guilt, shame and fear of abandonment do not necessarily have to happen. We see others doing the same thing without being criticized or abused. As we experience this gift of total acceptance, we feel a power in the room the likes of which we have never felt before. It is a power greater than ourselves. Many people in 12-step groups simply accept this kind of power as their Higher Power for years.

For many more people, this ability to be in relationship with a group of other human beings eventually opens the door to trusting that it is okay to be in relationship with something even more powerful than the group. Many people call this entity God. But the words and labels don't really matter. It is the relationship that matters, which is why it is God as we understand God, not as someone else understands God.

The spiritual healing that takes place during recovery brings us full circle back to the first stage of life: trust versus mistrust. With the ability to
trust that life is okay, that it will work out in the end even if it isn't pleasant
right now, we have wisdom. We have a sense of belonging. We have purpose
and meaning. We have choices.

And so as we heal deeper and deeper inside of ourselves, our lives become bigger and bigger and more connected with the lives of others outside
of ourselves. Recovery is thus about the expansion of the self out into the
universe, while at the same time, remaining humble and grateful that we are
sharing in creation.

Postlude

20

Kiss Your Monster
on the Nose

Once upon a time there was a little girl who lived in a village far from the big city. The village was nestled in a beautiful, sunlit valley surrounded by a tall snow-capped mountain range.

As the little girl grew older, she began to hike in the foothills at the base of the mountains. And when she became a teenager, she asked her parents if she could hike over the mountains to the village on the other side to visit her grandparents. At first, her parents were very upset and worried, and they told her that she could not go. But the little girl pleaded and begged and argued that someday she would be a young woman, and that she would have to grow up sometime. After several months of debate, her parents finally agreed to let her go.

Her father and mother taught her all that they knew about hiking and camping and surviving alone in the woods. They made her a backpack out of sturdy canvas, helped her pack, and then they all knelt down and prayed that she might have a safe journey. The next day she began her trek over the mountains.

Her first night alone was scary, but she managed to build a good fire, ate some of the sausage and cheese that her father had packed for her, and then fell asleep, covered by the soft quilts that her mother had made for her. The howling of the wolves frightened her a little, but she kept her fire burning brightly most of the night, which made her feel safer. The next day she awoke with the sun, ate her biscuits and jam while sunning herself on a big granite rock, then began hiking up the mountains. Late in the afternoon as the sun slipped behind the tops of the mountains, she reached a fork in the path. She did not know which way to go. Perplexed, she sat down and prayed for wisdom.

A few moments later she heard terrible frightening noises coming from the direction of both paths. Her heart raced and her palms sweated. Suddenly, from both paths, two monsters appeared. They were growling, gurgling, grumbling and snorting. The little girl grabbed her backpack and began to run down the hill, back toward her village. And then something inside of her told her to stop.

"Other people have hiked over these mountains and returned to tell about it," she thought to herself. "Maybe I'd better go back and see what this is all about."

The little girl stopped and turned around. The monsters had stopped right at the fork in the road, and something told her that they were trying to communicate with her. Slowly and carefully she walked back toward the monsters.

As she got closer, the monster guarding the path on the left said, "Take this path. It is much safer, and much quicker. Take this path and you'll see your grandparents tomorrow night."

At that very moment, the monster guarding the path on the right began to screech and howl a horrible blood-curdling howl. Fire belched from its mouth; smoke poured from its nose. The little girl was terribly frightened!

She bolted toward the monster on the left! As she got closer, she noticed that the monster on the left was not as ugly as the one on the right; and it was definitely not as scary. The closer she came to the one on the left, the louder the one on the right howled. She was so confused that she did not know what to do.

The monster on the left spoke in a soft voice, "Trust me. I am not as ugly as that other monster. And I do not make those disgusting noises." With that, the monster on the right screamed and gurgled and snorted and puffed even more. She began to take the path to the left, fearful even more that if she did not hurry, the other monster would chase after her and tear her to shreds.

A few hundred yards down the left path she looked back to see if the other monster was chasing her. It was still standing at the fork in the path, and it was screaming and howling more and more. But it was not chasing her. And then she stopped. The monster on the left path was walking a few steps ahead of her, and it just smiled at her, somewhat condescendingly, as if to say, "Don't be a fool."

And then something inside of her told her to go back and take the right path. The closer she came to the fork in the road, the faster she ran, until only seconds later, she was running down the right path and up into the mountains. She didn't know why she had made this choice, but she just kept going. As the last bit of twilight drifted into the blackness of night, she looked down the mountainside from whence she had come. She could see the fork in the path, and she could see the path she had taken as well as the one that she almost took.

Then she heard a thundering, rumbling, smashing, crashing, crushing sound that came from the left side of the mountain. Straining to see in the near-darkness, she saw a huge section of the mountain break loose and hurtle toward the left path below. Tons of rock and earth obliterated the left path at precisely the time that she would have been there had she gone that way. She fell to the ground and cried, releasing all the anxiety and tension of the past few hours.

Then, just a few feet in front of her appeared the ugly monster who had been guarding the right path. She looked up and gazed into its eyes. It was not howling and grumbling at all. Its eyes seemed peaceful and deep. Its face had softened into a compassionate gaze. Without knowing why, the little girl jumped up and kissed the monster on the nose! The monster blushed, and smiled.

"My name is Fear," said the monster, "and that other one's name is Destruction. If you run away from me without listening to what I have to say, you might end up avoiding something that is important for you. But if you listen to me just right, and learn to make friends with me, then you will have Wisdom. As for the monster guarding the left path, no matter how attractive it seems on the surface, nothing good ever comes from Destruction."

The little girl completed her journey after visiting her grandparents. Safely home in her own village, her parents noticed something very different about her. She was a young woman now, who had learned to make friends with her Fear, instead of being paralyzed or destroyed by it.

References/
Bibliography

Adams, K. M. (1987). "Sexual Addiction and Covert Incest." *Focus on Chemically Dependent Families*, May/June 1987. Pompano Beach, Fl.: Health Communications, Inc.

Alcoholics Anonymous World Services (1985). **Fifty Years With Gratitude.** New York: Alcoholics Anonymous World Service, Inc.

Bach, G. R. & Deutsch, R. M. (1970). **Pairing.** New York: Peter H. Wyden, Inc.

Black, C. (1981). **It Will Never Happen to Me!** Denver: M.A.C. Publishers.

Bowen, M. (1978). **Family Therapy in Clinical Practice.** New York: Jason Aronsen.

Carnes, P. (1987) **Out of the Shadows.** Minneapolis: Compcare.

Cermak, T. L. (1986). **Diagnosing and Treating Co-Dependence.** Minneapolis: Johnson Institute Books.

Cooper, K. H. (1970). **The New Aerobics.** New York: M. Evans and Co.

DeMause, L. (1974). **The History of Childhood.** New York: Psychohistory Press.

Erikson, E. H. (1963). **Childhood and Society.** New York: W.W. Norton and Co.

Erikson, E. H. (1986). **Identity: Youth and Crisis.** New York: W. W. Norton and Co., Inc.

Forward, S., & Torres, J. (1986). **Men Who Hate Women and the Women Who Love Them. New** York: Bantam Books.

Fossum, M. A., & Mason, M. J. (1986). **Facing Shame: Families In Recovery.** New York, W. W. Norton & Company, Inc.

Friel, J. C. (1982). **Paradoxical Dependency.** St. Paul, Minnesota: Unpublished manuscript.

————. (1985). "Co-Dependency Assessment Inventory: A Preliminary Research Tool." *Focus on Family and Chemical Dependency,* May/ June 1985. Pompano Beach, Florida: Health Communications, Inc.

Friel, J. C., Subby, R. C., & Friel, L. D. (1985). **Co-Dependency and the Search for Identity: A Paradoxical Crisis.** Pompano Beach, FL: Health Communications, Inc.

Friel, J. C. & Friel, L. D. (1986). **Life on My Own Terms: Stress Addiction Recovery Guide.** Pompano Beach, FL: Health Communications, Inc.

Fry, R. (1987). Personal communication.

Gould, R. L. (1978). **Transformations: Growth and Change in Adult Life.** New York: Simon & Schuster, Inc.

Kaufman, G. (1980). **Shame: The Power of Caring.** Cambridge, MA Schenkman Publishing Company.

Kellogg, T. (1986). **Return to Intimacy: Part One.** Excelsior, MN: Audio Cassette series by Terry Kellogg.

Kohn, A. (1987). "Shattered Innocence." *Psychology Today,* February, 1987: American Psychological Association.

Levinson, D. J. (1978). **The Seasons of a Man's Life.** New York: Alfred A. Knopf, Inc.

McGoldrick, M., & Gersen, R. (1985). **Genograms in Family Assessment.** New York: W. W. Norton & Company.

Miller, A. (1983). **For Your Own Good: Hidden Cruelty in Child-Rearing and the Roots of Violence.** New York: Farrar, Strauss & Giroux.

Miller, A. (1984). **Thou Shalt Not Be Aware: Society's Betrayal of the Child.** New York, Farrar, Strauss & Giroux.

Minuchin, S. (1974). **Families and Family Therapy.** Cambridge, MA: Harvard University Press.

Norwood, R. (1985). **Women Who Love Too Much: When You Keep Wishing and Hoping He'll Change.** Los Angeles: Jeremy P. Tarcher.

Peck, M. S. (1978). **The Road Less Traveled: A New Psychology of Love, Traditional Values and Spiritual Growth.** New York: Simon & Schuster.

Rogers, C. (1973). **Becoming Partners: Marriage and Its Alternatives.** New York: Delta Books.

Satir, V. (1967). **Conjoint Family Therapy.** Palo Alto, Ca.: Science and Behavior Books.

Sheehy, G. (1974). **Passages: Predictable Crises of Adult Life.** New York, E. P. Dutton.

Subby, R. C., & Friel, J. C. (1984). **Co-Dependency and Family Rules: A Paradoxical Dependency.** Pompano Beach, Florida: Health Communications, Inc.

Subby, R. C. (1987). Lost **in the Shuffle: The** Co-Dependent Reality. Pompano Beach, FL: Health Communications, Inc.

Turner, J. S. & Helms, D. D. (1987). **Lifespan Development** (Third Edition). New York: Holt, Rinehart, & Winston.

Wegscheider, S. (1981). **Another Chance: Hope and Help for the Alcoholic Family.** Palo Alto, CA: Science and Behavior Books.

Wholey, D. (1984). **The Courage To Change.** Boston: Houghton Mifflin.

Woititz, J. G. (1983). **Adult Children of Alcoholics.** Pompano Beach, FL: Health Communications, Inc.

Woititz, J. G. (1985). **Struggle for Intimacy.** Pompano Beach, FL: Health Communications, Inc.

Appendix

12-Step and Other Anonymous Groups

It seems that a month does not pass by without another 12-step or Anonymous Group starting up somewhere around the country. Once you have attended one Anonymous meeting, you will become part of a network of literally millions of people who are seeking their own recoveries, and who will be able to tell you about other Anonymous groups in your area.

These groups are free self-help groups. Most of them follow programs based on the original 12 steps of Alcoholics Anonymous. You are not required to speak during these groups unless you choose to do so, other than to give your first name. We have had many people who have attended these groups for as long as three to six months before they were comfortable talking. Being there is participation in the group. If you are afraid to go to your first meeting alone, as so many of us were, you can contact the group by telephone and someone will gladly accompany you.

To find a group in your area, the first thing to do is look in the white pages of your telephone directory. For example, most cities in the United States have a listing for Alcoholics Anonymous Intergroup or Information Services. If you call that number, someone will answer questions you have about meeting times and locations, where you can get more immediate help, etc.

The same is true for Al-Anon, Overeaters Anonymous and several others. For some of the newer groups, you may have to contact your local Mental Health Center or a clinic that specializes in family systems, addictions, co-dependency or adult children. Hospitals are usually good resources, too, because many of them now have chemical dependency treatment programs.